# Advantage Mr Christian

# Advantage
# Mr Christian

RICHARD BEWES

LUTTERWORTH PRESS
GUILDFORD AND LONDON

ISBN 0 7188 2105 X

Printed in Great Britain by
Cox & Wyman Ltd, London, Fakenham and Reading

# CONTENTS

# CONTENTS

# AUTHOR'S INTRODUCTION

My thanks are expressed to those who have helped me in the writing of this book. I am especially grateful to my former colleague Shelagh Horsman, who spent many hours in typing the manuscript at a time when I was immersed in the task of switching my job from one part of London to another.

Several chapters take the form of a story, and feature the introduction of various fictitious individuals. I need hardly say that such characters are genuinely fictitious, excepting in chapter four which explains itself.

My thanks are also due to two former colleagues, Roger and Robert, with whom I once shared a room during a conference that is now best forgotten. For me the most memorable part of the proceedings was a late night discussion that we held together in our room after a particularly depressing session. The idea for this book was sparked off as a direct result.

RICHARD BEWES

# I

## SOLD A LIE

The day had been a particularly heavy one for Stewart Dyson. He had kissed Joan good-bye earlier than usual, as he left his house in Woking that January morning. Clearing up the paper work at the office in Holborn was one contributing factor. It was a time-consuming chore that had to be completed before each of these bi-monthly business trips, and today had been no exception. Then he'd had to tie things up with the other heads of department and have a last-minute briefing before his departure.

The managing director had called him in during the morning, and had impressed on him the commissioning date of the big new communications project in East Africa, of which Stewart was now in charge. There was the question of the time scale. Not to mention the politics of the operation. Any delay in the setting up of the new satellite ground station was bound to affect relationships with the African politicians, and Stewart was made well aware of this.

He'd managed to grab a sandwich over the lunch hour, while he talked with his deputy about the vital points of the Saudi Arabian project that needed watching during his eight-day absence. The costs there had to be closely monitored if the contract was to be profitable. And there was always a possibility that the man in the field might foul things up with his limited experience in a big and involved scheme like this.

He'd spent the bulk of the afternoon going over the thick sheaf of papers that his secretary had been preparing for him over the past week. There was the latest issue of drawings sent down by the factory, together with a bundle of brochures of new equipment, and releases of up-to-date technical information. His itinerary had been finalized by his secretary, and she had given him all the telephone numbers of the strategic contacts he would be making. The British commercial attaché at the embassy. The chief of the Posts, Telephone and Telegraph Department. The manager at the Barclays D.C.&O.

He'd snapped his brief-case shut, and taken a taxi to Heathrow. An hour's run, and with a bit of luck he'd still have enough time to get himself a snack at the airport – maybe buy a few presents before boarding the British Airways flight for Nairobi. That is, if the London rush hour didn't hold him up. The Cromwell Road came into view. He fretted a little as the taxi halted in the heavy traffic. Only a few hours now, and he'd be in the January sunshine of Nairobi. The Hammersmith flyover slid by. Time was a bit tight after all now – it looked as if he'd have to forego the snack. Pity Joan couldn't be joining him – he'd have enjoyed taking her into Kenya's national game reserve. The M4 loomed ahead. Passport, ticket, travellers' cheques – everything was there. After all, you didn't become chief project engineer of the company's export department without getting a competent secretary.

Terminal 3. Pity, the time had gone. No time even for a drink. Check in, get rid of the suit-case – he'd need the brief-case for the flight – passport control, and into the departure lounge. A few minutes, and then his flight was being called. He made his way to gate 11, through the security check, and into the economy section of the jumbo jet.

His seat was in the non-smoking zone on the left-hand side. It was easier there, provided the plane wasn't full, as the seats that side were three abreast; he'd have room to open his brief-case on the centre seat. The window place was already occupied as he settled himself down for the first leg of the flight – to Zurich. He duly opened his brief-case, and went carefully through the contents, checking again on the documents, and refreshing his mind with the intricate details that would require his attention for the next eight days.

An hour after take-off found him satisfied that all was in order, and for the first time that day, Stewart Dyson began to relax. He ordered himself a black coffee, and presently became aware of his surroundings.

Over his brief-case he found himself exchanging pleasantries with an African of about his own age, thirty-five perhaps, who had been reading a copy of *Business Week*.

"Dropping off at Nairobi?" An East African as likely as not.

"That's right. I've been in England on a special study course."

"For long?"

"A year and a half. At the London School of Economics."

Gradually, as they chatted, Stewart found out more about his fellow-passenger. He was a Kenyan, a lecturer in economics at Nairobi University, and his name was Eddy Gachigi. A Kikuyu-sounding name, thought Stewart, recollecting some of his business associates in the Kenyan capital. His mind was in neutral now, operating efficiently on two levels, the pressures of the day eased, leaving his inner thoughts free to roam at will, while outwardly he maintained a competent conversation. The African was seeking information about the new communication system, details of which had recently broken in the papers, and Stewart willingly obliged.

"It's a pretty tightly wired world now," he remarked. "For quite a while of course we've been able to transmit the major events from Europe and America via satellite to most parts of the world. But who would ever have thought fifty years ago that we'd be doing a global transmission, live and in colour, of that heavyweight fight between Muhammed Ali and George Foreman direct from the heart of Zaire – or the Congo as they called it then? Remember that time? David Livingstone would have eaten his mosquito boots!"

"Times have certainly changed since then," smiled Eddy Gachigi, "even if they're less tranquil than they used to be. And maybe TV hasn't altogether helped there," he added.

"True," nodded Stewart absently. He must get off on the right foot with the chief of P.T.T. tomorrow, he reminded himself. The first five minutes of the meeting would be the most important. There was a selling job to do. He'd have to conceal the fact that the company was two months behind schedule. He could admit to a month perhaps . . .

Eddy was still talking. "I remember Malcolm Muggeridge, once comparing our present situation to a rather unpleasant experiment conducted by some scientists, who put a number of frogs into a bowl of water."

"And?" prompted Stewart.

"The water's temperature was very gradually raised to boiling point," continued Eddy, "but it was done so imperceptibly that none of the frogs made any real attempt to escape. Muggeridge was suggesting that today *we* are the frogs, and that we are being conditioned very gradually by the media – so gradually in fact, that we're largely unaware of the steady deterioration in our values and standards. And that boiling point is virtually upon us now!"

"And I suppose he said all this on TV?" grinned Stewart.

"Actually no. He was speaking at the 1974 World Congress on Evangelization, in Lausanne," corrected Eddy.

"Were you there yourself?" Stewart wanted to know.

"Yes. As an East African participant."

"I must confess I hadn't heard of it," admitted Stewart. "Were there many there?"

"Three or four thousand, I think. From about a hundred and fifty nations."

"Sounds a pretty representative collection of people," murmured Stewart. "You don't hear so much about Christianity in England these days. And what you do hear about it hardly seems in danger of setting the world on fire."

"But then isn't that partly because all these media people are believing their own propaganda?" countered the African. "You take the TV clergyman. The image he's invariably given in England is the same—"

"A simpering, gutless drip," agreed Stewart. "Granted, it's a caricature. But what about these 'Gift Day' appeals outside churches – when all you see is a lone clerical figure sitting at a table outside the porch, dolefully rattling a tin at the passers-by? And I remember when we did once take the children to a church service when we were on holiday in Cornwall, our seven-year-old reacted to the sound of Anglican chanting by asking me, 'Daddy, why do they *moan* here?' It's not that I disapprove of Christianity, exactly," added Stewart. "It's simply that so much of it – the buildings, the antiquity and bat-ridden graveyards – seems somehow allied to death."

"I feel a bit the same myself," admitted Eddy. "I became a Christian several years ago out in Africa, but everywhere in the West, I find the bland assumption that Christianity is on the retreat. After a while you find yourself half-believing that you've joined a cause which, though admirable, has a built-in failure factor."

The plane had now landed in Zurich, and conversation was suspended as the bulk of the passengers took the opportunity of the short break to stretch their legs in the airport transit lounge. A curious thing, reflected Stewart Dyson as he browsed at the news stand in the lounge, that he should find himself baring his soul to an African stranger on the subject of religion. Perhaps the fact that he *was* an African had something to do with it. And of course they would never meet again . . .

A meal was served on the second leg of the flight, and Stewart was occupied for a while with a prawn cocktail, followed by steak, sauté potatoes and peas. Finishing his fruit salad, he turned once more to his companion.

"This 'failure factor' that you were talking about," he ventured. "How can you keep your own beliefs intact when all around the things you stand for are crumbling?"

Eddy looked up from his book. "Deep down I suppose I know that they're not crumbling – that's probably it," he explained. "A lot of the dead wood is being cleared out of modern Christianity – particularly in the West. I for one welcome that. But the idea that Christianity as such is now dead is a lie that's been repeated throughout history. The lie may be swallowed blithely by millions today, but that's no new thing either."

"But even assuming it isn't dead," objected Stewart, "the fact remains that it has about as much chance of making a dent in today's world, as a nutcracker with a centurion tank."

"Well, the Emperor Diocletian once thought that," answered the African. "Back at the turn of the third century he evidently believed that he was living in the 'post-Christian era', because he even had a special badge made, to celebrate the demise of the Church! Apparently the boast inscribed on the medal was 'The Christian religion is destroyed, and the worship of the gods is restored', but in the last analysis it was the Roman Empire that bit the dust, while the Christian cause plodded on."

"But always this fragile picture," persisted Stewart, sipping his coffee.

"You're right there," said Eddy. "The Christian cause has never thrived on the big civic receptions, banner headlines or ticker-tape parades. Maybe this is why the media fails to capture the true picture."

"There was that series of documentaries that the BBC ran some years ago on the British Empire," remarked Stewart. "I remember that when they were dealing with the work of foreign missionaries, the impression given was one of almost total failure in places like Africa, and that you lot were fast reverting to heathenism. True or false?"

"Well, however much we may have failed," said Eddy, "the facts, untrumpeted and unheralded as they are, are that there are more African and Asian Christians in the world today than there are European. We're seeing plenty of expansion today in Kenya! And next door in central Tanzania, they're putting up one new church building *every seven days* – and they've been maintaining that rate for over fifteen years!"

Stewart Dyson was impressed in spite of himself.

"Another thing," went on Eddy, "a whole lot of churches in England may have their backs to the wall, and some are closing down – but you've got a purer church as a result. There's more warmth and acceptance around the place than there's been for decades. And look at the young life in the universities and youth organizations! And the deluge of Christian books that roll off your presses. I maintain that England today is still one of the easiest places in the world in which to become a Christian."

"If one *wanted* to be a Christian," rejoined Stewart slowly. "But I'm not sure that I really believe in God in the first place, Eddy."

"Fair enough," countered Eddy. "What *do* you believe then?"

"About what?"

"About life on this world? What is your own world-view?"

"I'm not sure that I have one."

"You must have, Stewart. Every man has a world-view."

There was a pause in the conversation as the film show began in the spacious passenger cabin. Stewart and Eddy chose to ignore it, leaving their headsets at the side of their seats. Stewart glanced at his watch. It was nearly midnight.

"Sorry Eddy. Keep going," he prompted.

Eddy Gachigi thought for a moment before speaking.

"I think," he said soberly, "that defeatism or loss of direction hits an individual when he starts to believe the world's lies. My own view is that the world has sold us not one lie, but a tissue of lies. It may be the hard sell of blatant materialism one day, or the soft sell of half-baked theories of dubious scholarship the next. You know, the sort of stuff that turns up in the Sunday press – Easter day 'revelations', the flying saucers of Ezekiel, mushroom myths and so on."

Stewart lifted an eyebrow. "Sounds like a load of old fungus," he observed mildly.

"Of course," agreed Eddy. "The fact remains that if a man won't believe the Gospel, he may allow himself to believe – anything. My own Christian world-view is bound to suffer once I let the world's con-tricks get a hold on me. But one of the problems in staying afloat as a Christian these days is time."

Eddy looked at his companion. "We are both very busy people," he stated quietly. "So busy, that we find it all too easy to let life take its course, without ever bothering to *think*. Do you know Gordon Bailey's poem, *Plastic World*?"

Stewart shook his head.

"I have it here." Eddy rummaged in his wallet, and pulled out a clipping from a magazine. He handed it over, and Stewart read silently:

*The booths of the gipsies : the screams of the gay,*
*The lights and the laughter all drag you their way ;*
*The hopes of a win and some semblance of fun*
*Help cover the fact that you've really been done.*
*The rifles are fixed and the arrows are bent ;*
*The coconuts seem to be set in cement . . .*
*A cheap plastic world full of cheap plastic toys*
*Where polythene girls cling to polythene boys ;*
*Transparent and flimsy, creation gone wrong—*
*A make-believe happiness made in Hong Kong.*

Stewart looked over at Eddy. "Keep it," smiled the

African. "A piece of philosophy to help you in your business tomorrow."

"It's tomorrow already," replied Stewart, looking again at his watch. He pocketed the scrap of paper. "Let's meet again," he suggested. "I've got eight days in Nairobi. We could continue our conversation. Come and lunch with me at the New Stanley in a couple of days."

"Delighted," said Eddy. "And now if you don't mind, I'm going to get an hour or two of sleep."

They composed themselves, and the jumbo jet roared on over the Sahara, the African and the Englishman side by side in peaceful oblivion within the air-conditioned cabin. One in economics, the other in exports. And both extremely busy.

\* \* \*

Not that you can leave it there, of course. It isn't enough merely to expose a lie. For the verdict of history is that the most exciting way to live is God's way. Today's Christian needs reminding that the advantage lies with him in the pressures that confront him in the current scene. He is required to do battle with evil and darkness in the time of greatest change that the world has ever known – but he belongs to the winning side in virtue of his allegiance to the most exciting, the most magnetic personality ever to enter our planet's history. How to manage and how to win, amid today's complexities, as a disciple of Christ – the great Winner – would be, perhaps, rather a pretentious aim for a little book like this. But at least there may be some encouragements to pick up along the way.

## 2

## TAKING LIFE BY THE THROAT

It was the night of the election results. Of the all-night vigil with Hardiman Scott. But not for me. Me, I had other fish to fry. Pancho Gonzales was playing Rod Laver in the final of the BBC2 Tennis Professional Masters Tournament at Wembley, and I was determined to see the historic encounter on the "Box".

The trouble was, we hadn't got BBC2 on our television set. "I'll give Fred Hurding a buzz," I thought. At the time Fred Hurding was a member of our church in Essex, one of those marvellous characters that only East London can produce. Stories about him abounded, mostly concerning the glorious bricks he dropped as he wended his genial way through life. "The first reading is taken from the letter to the Ethiopians," was his mystifying introduction once to the Sunday lesson in church. And people loved him for it.

I dialled his number.

"Fred?"

"Hullo, that you, Richard?"

"Yes, look Fred, Gonzales is playing Laver on BBC2 tonight, would it be all right if we came round to see it with you on your set?"

I thought at the time that Fred sounded a trifle hesitant.

"Er – yes, that would be f-fine, we'd love to see Gonzales playing; come right over." Fred, of course, had never heard of the immortal Gonzales, was probably expecting to see a game of chess or snooker as much as anything else, as he switched over from the election results to BBC2 while Mary his wife put on the coffee.

At the time I was unaware of Fred's passionate interest in the election, in all elections, and of his regular custom of sitting an election night through, camped over the TV set. On reflection I can see that the evening, for him, must have been one of excruciating frustration. The Gonzales–Laver duel fully lived up to its expectations. It was a long match, culminating in a protracted and tense final set. It dawned on me that as the players changed courts every two games, Fred would reach out, so very nonchalantly, to the TV switch, with the murmured comment "Might just as well see how the election's getting along on the other channel shall we?" Then Mary, ever tactful, would gently prod him. "Now let's get back to the tennis, Fred. That's what we really want to see." "Er, yes," Fred would gulp obediently. And so the match wound tortuously on.

Laver was at his shining best. The great Gonzales, of course, was well over his peak, knocking on forty, and it was a question of whether he could harbour his stamina sufficiently to subdue the brilliant Laver before his legs gave out. In between games I gravely shared my doubts with my hosts – against a slightly tiresome background noise of politics emanating from the telly. Some nonsense about a close finish at Billericay. Or was it Havering? Mary tactfully eased the switch again. Match point – to Gonzales! An eternity of suspense followed, and suddenly it was over – the roar of applause from the Wembley crowd cut off in a flash by the smooth confident voice of Hardiman Scott – "News now in a marginal seat of a Labour gain." Fred's itching fingers had reached out once more.

"Very many thanks, Fred and Mary, we did enjoy the evening."

"Not a bit, Richard, come again won't you." (*Thinks* But not at Election time!)

\* \* \*

In our family we had a multitude of interests as children, but my favourite was undeniably tennis. I made scrapbooks, I obtained autographs, I played in tournaments, I slept on the pavement to see Wimbledon finals – and Gonzales was my schoolboy hero. The enthusiasm was infectious too. Paul Wigram, the son of Kenya missionaries, came to live with us for some months in our Blackheath home. Before long he was as mesmerized as the rest of us.

"Auntie Sylvia, I'm sorry, but I've broken an electric light bulb."

"Never mind, Paul, we'll put in a new one. Which room was it in?"

"In the lavatory."

22

"In the—" Calmly, "But how did you break it in there of all places?"

"Just practising my serve!" ...

\* \* \*

So I had my tennis. Some people collect stamps, and others go pot-holing. What of it? Although such pastimes are a fascinating feature of life, nobody could ever convince me that the pursuit of such activities – however absorbing – could be anything more than a fascinating sideline of life itself. The real thing, that is.

Behind the various pursuits of our family in those earlier days lay the altogether stronger and binding factor of our common faith. By that I do not mean that we were always talking of religious subjects, any more than we were growing up as little plaster saints. Mercifully we children were free from being nagged, goaded and "challenged" at home about our spiritual progress. Such moments of confrontation tended to come from outside.

But there were the reminders. Constantly, all around us and every day. Not simply during grace at the breakfast table or at family prayers, though we had all of that! The reminders were coming at us all the time in a variety of intangible ways – in tone of voice and laughter, in attitudes to possessions and money, in the daily interpretation of events and relationships. Reminders that life is more than pastimes – however enthusiastically pursued – more than food, drink, clothes and personal ambitions. There is something bigger, and that is discovering and establishing your relationship to the Universe. It is just here that materialism meets with devastating, crashing failure.

I remember seeing a TV documentary about the late Bertrand Russell. In a film clip he was seen reminiscing about his early childhood. He recalled, as a little boy of about seven, hearing the dying words of a close relation on his deathbed – I think it was his grandfather – "Good-bye, my darlings – for ever!"

For ever. It can be a terrifying thought, eternity. Lying mistily behind, stretching blankly ahead, while here, in the immediate present, is a man, a little candle flame flickering up for a few years before being snuffed out as the darkness rushes in. *For ever*. Logically that's how the humanist has to view the scene; man on his own, stripped of the dignity accorded him in the Bible as created in God's image, a freak happening on a green planet – itself a fluke phenomenon in a meaningless universe – jogging brightly, briefly along before plunging into oblivion.

This of course is the nightmare of modern man's depression. Drugs, the hippie culture, the current obsession with occultism, the Divine Light movement, are all part of a restless search for something better. But many today are finding Christ and discovering in him the key that finally unlocks the total puzzle and makes sense of the universe and of all existence. It is not that Christ is one of several workable alternatives. He stands alone:

Christ is the visible likeness of the invisible God. He is the first-born Son, superior to all created things.

For by him God created everything in heaven and on earth, the seen and the unseen things, including spiritual powers, lords, rulers, and authorities. God created the whole universe through him and for him. He existed before all things, and in union with him all things have their proper place. (Colossians 1: 15–17 TEV)

The term "Jesus" is flung around a good deal today, often as no more than a popular bandwaggon-type cliché used by some modern song-writers and various spin-off groups on the edge of the Christian scene. Devotees of the Guru Maharaj Ji, who arrived in England in 1973, acclaimed him as another Christ come again – a view totally at variance with the warnings uttered by the Christ of the Bible!

"Then if anyone says to you, 'Look, here is the Messiah!' or 'There he is!' – do not believe him. For false Messiahs and false prophets will appear; they will perform great signs and wonders, for the purpose of deceiving God's chosen people, if possible. Listen! I have told you this ahead of of time.

"Or, if people should tell you, 'Look he is out in the desert!' – don't go there; or if they say 'Look, he is hiding here!' – don't believe it . . ." (Matthew 24: 23–26 TEV)

Christ is more than a word; rather he is The Word – God's last Word to this planet.[1] When you have looked

[1] Hebrews 1: 2.

at the Man of Galilee, the Christ of our history, there is nowhere else to look; you've come to the end of the search; you're faced with someone who has outlasted every trendy fashion and philosophy. Cliff Richard expresses it well in a song of his own:

*I read in the paper that you were back in fashion;*
*Amongst famous men, you are high on the list.*
*Won't they realize that fashions are passing fancies?*
*The truth is, yesterday, today, for ever you're unchanging,*
*Yesterday, today, for ever, never wavering;*
*You stated who you were, and that will never change,*
*Like it or not, you'll always be the same – Son of God.*

Christ is the key to the whole thing. Here is the historical God-Man, who claimed "I am the way, the truth and the life; No one comes to the Father, but by me".[1] Without him, even the most brilliant men are reduced to virtually blind guesswork when trying to establish the existence and the nature of God.

Elizabeth, my sister, used to read classics at Cambridge University. We asked her whether studying the ancient philosophers ever undermined her Christian faith. "Never," she'd firmly reply. "My faith was strengthened the more I read them. You'd see how tantalizingly near these old boys would get to the truth of God revealed in Jesus – so near that you'd say to yourself 'They must see it!' – but then at the last minute they'd veer away and miss the whole thing – completely. Studying the philosophers only emphasized to me how much we needed a revelation."

[1] John 14: 6.

26

And so to the all-important question "Who was or is this Jesus?" Was he a fraudulent fake, or was he mad in claiming to be Son of God and the way to God; or did he speak the truth? Those are the only three possible conclusions open to us. You cannot, for example, say "He was the best man who ever lived, but just a man", without saying in the same breath that he was a liar – or a madman; for Jesus' main statements were about himself, his role and his relationship to the Father. If he is wrong in his central claims, he is not simply mistaken – he has to be mad, such was the breathtaking audacity of statements like "He who has seen me has seen the Father",[1] or "Whoever lives and believes in me shall never die".[2]

It never ceases to amaze me that so much speculation about the possibility of an after-life fails to take into account what is at least the claim that a man came back from death to be its everlasting Conqueror. It's a sheer waste of time to speculate about the other side of death until *that* has been looked into! Just for a start, you can take the empty tomb, the reported appearances, and the changed disciples. But there is more to it than that.

After all, others have apparently "died", and made a comeback. Even to the extent of being nailed down in the coffin first! But how long does the excitement last? I can (just) remember such an occurrence in 1969. A man had died, and come back to life again. The item barely squeezed into the BBC *World at One* programme. I never saw it featured in any paper. The man's

[1] John 14: 9.
[2] John 11: 26.

name? I forgot it within minutes of the programme's end. Presumably it will be on a gravestone one day.

If Jesus had not risen from the grave – clearly and unequivocally as the Conqueror of Death for all mankind – *we would never have heard of him.* The demoralized movement comprising eleven scared men would have fizzled out on the launching pad. Why didn't it fizzle out? *That*'s got to be looked into! There are altogether too many problems encountered in dismissing the Bible narrative as phoney, for one's sense of integrity to remain intact. Start saying that Jesus hadn't actually died on the cross and that he revived later – and you have a whole bundle of problems on your hands, including the simple "When did he die then?" The arguments have all been well explored in that paperback classic *Who Moved the Stone*[1] by Frank Morison, a sceptic who began writing with the determination to explode the "myth" of Jesus' resurrection only to wind up totally convinced of the story's literal truth.

Such an investigation is vital, because if Christ is who he says he is, then, frankly the long nightmare of modern man's quest is over. Problems there may be, but the main questions are answered. The jig-saw puzzle about man's origin, purpose and significance in this universe is finally completed.

It's altogether too important an issue *not* to be considered. The fear that many have of being caught up finally by their failures and sins at a future Day of Reckoning after death melts away to nothing in the face of the sacrifice of the cross and the assurance

[1] Morison, F. *Who Moved the Stone?* Faber & Faber Ltd.

of one who said he had come "to seek and to save the lost".

Let me put it this way. I have a nightmare dream once every few months. And my nightmare is just this – that I find myself back at university about to take my final exams all over again! I am, of course, caught out, totally unready. In my dream I know that something is wrong – I find myself thinking "I shouldn't be here – I know I'm a minister somewhere – perhaps it's simply a dream". But I don't seem to wake up, and the moment of reckoning draws ever closer.

And then I do wake up! I can only say that the sense of relief is indescribable. I lie there in the darkness hugging the amazing truth to myself. It's all right. *It's all right.* It happened way back all those years ago. I passed!

But come to another nightmare, your nightmare. The final examinations are upon you. And there you are, a miserable individual, unready, caught out. You walk into the examination hall, sit down at the desk and pick up the question paper. A single glance confirms your worst fears. You're doomed. Not even a single question can you attempt. Your knees turn to jelly and your stomach turns over with fright. Just then there's a tap on your shoulder, as an insignificant looking little man in spectacles murmurs in your ear "Excuse me sir, you shouldn't be here".

"Shouldn't be here?"

"No sir, you don't have to take this examination. You see, you've already passed."

"Passed?" The room sways around you.

"Yes," comes the confident reply. "Our records

indicate that you've already passed; look!" and a scroll of paper is whipped in front of you.

"Your degree," explains the small gentleman. "You shouldn't be here at all. You've already passed; you can go."

And slowly you stumble out of the examination hall into the brilliant sunshine of a wonderful June morning, dazedly clutching the degree that you never deserved. Gradually the amazing truth sinks in. Unbelievably, you've passed! But all this is only a pale reflection of the Gospel itself. Jesus expressed it as follows (Phillips version):

"I solemnly assure you that the man who hears what I have to say and believes in the One who has sent Me, has eternal life. He does not have to face judgment; he has already passed from death to life." (John 5: 24)

The Gospel itself, then, what is it? It is a pronouncement to the believer, here and now, of the future verdict of the Judgment upon him! He is declared as having already passed from death to life, as being already accepted, already forgiven, the present possessor of eternal life. And all because Jesus came, died upon the cross for him, and rose again.

"It sounds too good to be true," a young person said to me once. "Tell it to me all over again – slowly." And I did.

Clearly this kind of belief has to be more than an "enthusiasm". The person who is simply playing at Christianity plays equally at a number of other pursuits, the new conservatory, Saturday afternoon football, the local meeting of the Rotary. Step the pressure up a little, let him fall out with a member of his church, let him move to a new area – and he'll be off. He's never really seen Christ at all.

To become a real Christian is to grapple with the biggest issues of all – to take life itself by the throat. The decision a person makes about Jesus Christ affects not only his whole outlook and way of life, but may well have a decisive bearing upon the destiny of the next generation.

On the evening of Tuesday, September 26, 1882, a fourteen-year-old boy in Plymouth sat listening to the celebrated American evangelist, D. L. Moody. The youngest of twelve children, Tommy was evidently unable to get any of the rest of the family to come with him to Plymouth's Guild Hall, so it is not clear who accompanied him that night. At any rate, the next Friday, he wrote a letter to one of his sisters, in the following terms:

My dear Evy,

   I am writing to tell you some good news which you will be glad to hear. I went to one of Moody and Sankey's meetings on Tuesday and there *I was saved*. He spoke from the ninth verse of the third of Genesis. It is: Where art thou? He said that that was the first question that God ever asked man in the Bible, and that it was the first question that people ought to ask themselves and he said that there were two more that he was going to speak about and they were: Where are you going?

and How are you going to spend eternity? I don't think he could have chosen better ones.

That Tommy's decision was no flash in the pan was evidenced by his later emergence as a man of Christian stature and leadership in the Church of God. Also by the fact that over the decades his whole family, virtually to a man, was to become involved in Christ's cause through his prayers and example – right down to today's grandchildren and great-grandchildren. I ought to know because Tommy Bewes was my grandpa.

And the moral of that is: be careful when you think to reach out and take life – real life – by the throat. It may turn around and seize you instead.

# 3

## INVISIBLE CHAINS

"Your turn, Daddy."

"Right," I said, "I've thought of someone."

"Alive or dead?"

"Well" – I hesitated. The trouble was, I'd thought of Humpy Dumpty.

That's the pattern of those games, when you're bombing up the M1 with a lively family. After a bit, you've done everybody, Granny, Zaachaeus, Evonne Goolagong, Tom and Jerry, each character exercising its own peculiar fascination and invisible pull upon young minds.

Everything is in such a jumble at that stage of life. Nursery rhymes tend to get chosen in the Christian chorus slot at the Sunday School. Gradually the tangle gets sorted out, fact from fantasy, history from fiction, the important from the trivial. This sifting is, of course, a lifetime process, taking place continuously at most levels of life and work.

Before I had a secretary, I had several letter trays in

my office that purported to sort out my correspond-
ence. One was marked "Read". Into it I simply popped
anything that defeated me. Needless to say it was bulg-
ing. If my colleagues were at a loss to discover some
missing form or memorandum, they usually had a little
rummage in "Read", and eureka, the thing would turn
up. It became quite a joke in the end. An undesirable
letter from some faceless official in London would
arrive – landing me with an impossible time-consuming
chore – and I'd take it out on the poor man by cheerfully
banishing him to "Read".

Spiritual issues are not exempt from this kind of
avoiding action of course. In most people's minds there
are compartments marked "Pending", "Irrelevant",
or even "Not worth considering", and frequently the
things of God are consigned to these pigeon holes, the
sorting out, growing-up process tragically halted. I
recall the words of Lord Boothby during an *Any
Questions* radio programme. The topic under con-
sideration was the After Life. "The thought of a
spiritual Boothby twanging a spiritual harp for eternity
has, for me, limited attractions." Even allowing that the
words were spoken in jest, they told us more about
Lord Boothby than about heaven. The impression
given was that he had never seriously considered the
subject.

The truth is that the rate of a person's spiritual
progress has nothing whatever to do with his IQ.
In a prayer, our Lord once acknowledged that – "You
have shown to the unlearned what you have hidden
from the wise and learned".[1] It is not that a man of high

[1] Matthew 11: 25 (TEV).

intelligence and academic attainment *cannot* be a member of God's Kingdom; there are plenty of such who are Christians today. It is simply that a high intelligence in itself has no bearing on the question any more than the "niceness" of an individual. It would be very unfair if it were otherwise! After all, some people are born intelligent, while others are less gifted. Most sunny-natured people inherit their "niceness", and the morose quiet personalities are similarly naturally endowed with their temperaments. It's no credit to a person either way.

When, as a teenager, I went to my first-ever Christian holiday houseparty, I found my thinking challenged on this very point. Of course I'd had a Christian upbringing. Somehow I was imagining that a decent kind of life with a church background would carry me through. Michael my brother and I shared a bedroom with several others in the houseparty. We were already prepared for the fact that it was a religious show and that there would be prayers. And if it came to any of the houseparty leaders attempting a serious conversation with either of us ... well we could take care of that too. Without a word being exchanged on the subject there was a silent understanding between us that we would take avoiding action. A leader would stride purposefully in our direction and we would turn to each other.

"How about a game of clock golf?"

"I don't mind."

"It's over here I think."

And we'd slope off together leaving the luckless pursuer in our wake, scalpless.

It was a very carefree time of life for us both. Examinations hadn't reached the high-powered stage that they had for my older brother, Peter – who was also at that houseparty and a committed Christian already. It was around that period that the era of the West Indian calypsos began. I can still recall the absurd words of *The Chinese Cricket Match*, which we three brothers used to sing at odd moments, in what we prided ourselves were authentic West Indian accents:

*It's Yin Sing, caught and bowled by Loompan and Ring
   Ting;*
*Clean bowled by Poompan –*
*And the whole grandstand SHOUT*
*When Loopan, Pootwang, Poomping, Pooning – OUT!*

But back to the houseparty. What finally got me was a talk on about the fourth night at the evening prayers session. The speaker was majoring on the theme that Christianity is a relationship – a friendship with a Person, Jesus Christ. And that this Jesus desired, by his invisible presence – the Holy Spirit – to enter our lives and personalities, and to begin a friendship with us which would continue for ever. I had heard it all before, but somehow tonight there was a fresh urgency about the message. How could this friendship begin? I was all agog.

*There's a way back to God from the darkness of sin,*
*There's a door that is open, and you may go in;*
*At Calvary's Cross is where you begin,*
*When you come as a sinner to Jesus.*

The words had already been sung at the houseparty and now the speaker emphasized their meaning as he talked about the death of Christ for our sins. Up till then I'd never really understood the cross. I knew the story well, but the penny had never dropped. I began to see that there was more to the story than the thorns, and the nails and the thirst. Here was God coming down as Man among us, perfect and guiltless, to take upon himself the guilt of our sins that would otherwise keep us from heaven. Here was Christ the Saviour undergoing the banishment from the Father that I deserved as he cried, "My God, my God, why have you forsaken me?" All so that we could go free, that I could be forgiven and accepted, in short, treated as though I had never sinned at all!

The cross is the answer to man's belief that he can gain God's favour by a do-it-yourself approach. Religious observance, greater moral effort, believing the right doctrines – none of these can gain us a step nearer God. *If they could, Jesus would never have gone to the cross.* For he prayed in the Garden of Gethsemane before his ordeal "My Father, *if it be possible*, let this cup pass from me; nevertheless not as I will, but as you will."[1] But Christ went to Calvary. Thus for a man to insist that he can find the way to acceptance with God by his own self-effort is to hurl an insult into the face of Christ – is to say to him – "You didn't need to die – I've got there on my own without your help."

The quiet voice of the speaker continued with the talk. "You think then, that there's nothing for you to do at all – that forgiveness is yours automatically? But that

[1] Matthew 26: 39.

wouldn't be your attitude with any other gift. For eternal life is a gift you see. Supposing your uncle was to buy you a cricket bat, had paid for it already, and then instructed you to go and collect the parcel from the store? The bat wouldn't be yours until you'd collected it, claimed it for yourself."

It was the sort of illustration that the average schoolboy could understand, and I was no exception.

My attention was riveted as the talk came to a close. "The way to make Christ's gift your own is to accept him into your life," said the speaker. "Tell him you're sorry for your sins that took him to the cross. Admit your need of his forgiveness, and thank him for dying for you personally. Resolve that you are going unashamedly to let Christ be the Lord of your life from now on. Then simply, in a prayer of your own, open the door of your life to him."

My discussion of the evening with Michael the next day was barely necessary – I think we both knew that the other had taken an important step. "Discussion" actually is rather a polite word when I think of it:

"That talk last night, it was marvellous, wasn't it?"

"It was the best I've ever heard. Fantastic."

"Umm . . . How about a game of table bowls?"

Or something like that!

On the evening itself, nothing could have dissuaded me from the step that I knew I must take. The gathering broke up in its usual way. Talk and laughter. A few late night walks. Story swapping in the bedrooms. But all the time I was thinking, "I'm going to do what that man says, I'm going to pray that prayer that he was talking about. I'll do it tonight, late, when everything's quiet and people have gone to sleep."

I can't say in all honesty that I felt particularly "different" after my prayer of commitment. But somehow it did seem like the close of one chapter and the beginning of another.

# 4

## GAME, SET AND MATCH

"Don't you think that the impact of Good Friday and Easter on the world would make marvellous journalistic copy?" I once asked one of my colleagues, Robert Backhouse. We were being driven down the Southend arterial road by Shelagh Horsman, our highly versatile secretary, on our way through Essex to the printers in Rayleigh, to correct the church magazine proof. We flashed under the Upminster flyover.

"Mmm, why not?" agreed Robert. "After all, the main impact of Easter can be seen in two thousand years of Christian experience – right up to the present day. You know, human stories. That ought to make good material for any editor, oughtn't it?"

"It would present a unique challenge to a modern journalist," I went on. "In fact it wouldn't be beyond us to devise an imaginary report along those lines now, would it?"

"I'm sure it wouldn't," confirmed Robert. "Of

course the actual stories couldn't be imaginary. They'd have to be authentic."

I nodded in agreement. "Of course." The car sped on through Horndon . . .

*　　*　　*

Ken Lovett leaned back in his chair and meditatively doodled on his clip-board as he sat with his colleagues at the morning conference. Of stocky build, he was in his early forties, inclining a little to plumpness – the legacy of seventeen years of physical inertia. His only exercise was the brisk walk from Blackfriars Station that took him up to Ludgate Circus and into Fleet Street. He belonged to a golf club near his suburban home in Kent, but his promotion to assistant editor features three years back had made heavier inroads into his leisure time than he could have foreseen.

He looked up. "At any rate," he concluded defensively, "we've looked at all the possible follow-up ideas to the story of that suburban church that's causing all the stir. This one's seasonable if nothing else. After all, it is Easter next week. Let's see what kept the Church ticking when Christ was nailed to the cross – and how far it's ticking now." He stood up. "It's now Tuesday. That gives us a couple of days if we want to carry the feature on Thursday." He paused for a moment. *"The Church that refused to lie down* – that's the line we'll take. We could make it a double page spread. Miles Drury will cover the early historical research. Oliver Tomlinson can look for evidence that the Church really is alive today – we want stuff from all over the world, mind – and Bob Tipperton can dig out the human stories." The conference over, Lovett returned to his room, called in the writers and briefed them. Then, remembering he had to cash a cheque, he took advantage of the lull to slip out to the bank. He threaded his way through the open plan office, leaving the clatter of typewriters behind him as he took the lift down to the ground floor of the newspaper building. Miles Drury followed him out.

Back at his own desk Oliver Tomlinson unzipped his brief-case and pulled out a packed lunch. "A nice assignment for a feature writer!" he mumbled, biting into an egg sandwich, "just a little stuff from all over the world, Oliver old man!" He looked up. "Where the dickens am I going to start, Bobby?" He looked up accusingly over the top of his sandwich.

"Better start the other side of the world," grinned Bob Tipperton smugly. "Kick off with Japan, and get through to Jim Hocking over in Hokkaido. You might just get him before he turns in for the night!"

Lovett returned from the bank to finalize a feature on airport security for the Wednesday edition, and found that Miles Drury had already phoned a report through from Aldwych to the copy taker. He thumbed through the flimsy automatic carbons. "Young Miles doesn't waste time," he smiled to himself, "Blessed if he hasn't dug out that bit of early history from Tacitus during the lunch hour." He scanned another page and silently read the words of the aged second-century Bishop Polycarp. Urged by the Roman Proconsul to renounce Jesus Christ, the old man had replied: "*Eighty and six years have I served him, and he hath done me no wrong: how then can I blaspheme my King who saved me?*"

Lovett flipped over another carbon for the end of the story. "Burnt alive" he murmured. He gathered up the remaining pages and handed them to one of the features sub-editors. "Get this cut to length, would you, Jack – say six hundred words. Put it up for setting and give it some cross heads as you go." He turned back to his desk.

Later in the afternoon Bob Tipperton spoke to him. "I've got some stuff already for that Easter feature. One of the local boys in Erith out in Kent knows a youngish clergyman called Garth Grinham out at Northumberland Heath—"

"We don't want all clergymen," interrupted Lovett, looking over his teacup.

"No, I know. It's okay. It's just that this guy's given us a couple of stories. . . There's a girl called" – he began to read – "Hazel Aylward. She's a cancer case – a pretty bad one – now in her thirties." Lovett listened attentively as the story briefly unfolded. Hazel Aylward lived in a bungalow with her family in Erith. Was a convinced Christian. Didn't expect special treatment from the Almighty, in spite of her faith. When told to prepare herself for the biggest operation she had ever faced, she summoned up enough strength to reach out for her book of daily Bible readings, and found encouragement in the first sentence of the letter of Jude – "Kept for Jesus Christ". She had come through that operation, but her days seemed numbered and she knew it. She was content. No, she laid no blame on God. She trusted him implicitly, wanted all who were close to her to trust him too. In him she found confidence of victory over darkness and despair. She had a while to go yet . . .

"And there's this other one too," said Bob Tipperton, consulting his notes. "Her name's Mary Swan . . . born in 1952, lives in a semi-detached in Bexleyheath, and works in local government. She's been blind from birth, and apparently is an inspiration to all the members of Garth Grinham's church. She's a tennis fanatic, incidentally."

"Tennis?" queried Lovett. "She doesn't play, surely?"

"No. She follows the game. Goes to the Albert Hall for the Dewar Cup matches. Takes *Tennis World* magazine. Follows the history, studies the game. She's met some of the big names, Virginia Wade, Margaret Court, Nastase. Has plenty of interests. She says—" Bob looked down again – "She says, 'Easter Day means everything to me because it tells of new hope and eternal life'. I've got a bit more on her here."

Lovett reached over and took the sheets himself, stirring his tea absentmindedly as he read. He flipped through the pages and then looked up. "Good lad," he nodded. "That stuff's real all right. Get it subbed and up to the printer soon as you like. And now if you don't mind, I'd better have another look at tomorrow's piece . . ."

Oliver Tomlinson, impatient to see what was coming in from Japan, bent over and peered at the stuttering telex machine in the wire room. "Not bad, not bad, though I say it myself," he confided cheerfully to the only other two occupants of the little room, who eyed him without expression from their chairs, a motionless haze of cigarette smoke hanging above them. He turned again to the machine. "Here it all comes, straight from

Jim Hocking in Hokkaido – not bad for four hours' work, eh?" He paused a moment. "You two are about to hear the story of Captain Mitsuo Fuchida, the bright boy the Japs chose to lead the air attack on Pearl Harbor. Get an earful of this." There was silence behind him. Tomlinson bent a little closer to the machine, opened his mouth to speak, and then suddenly changed his mind. The two others could stew.

Mitsuo Fuchida's life had been changed through the story of an American girl who showed kindness to Japanese prisoners of war, in spite of the fact that her missionary parents had both been beheaded by the Japs at the outset of the war. "Where is it possible to find such love?" Fuchida wondered. His own personality was filled with bitterness and hate, and life seemed to hold no more meaning for him. He found the answer to his question when he was prompted to read the Bible for himself. On reading the story of Christ's sufferings at the hands of his enemies, Fuchida came to the words "Forgive them, Father! They don't know what they are doing". He now knew the source of the love that cannot be conquered. It lay in a living relationship with this Jesus. He accepted Christ immediately. Later he was to emerge as a Christian leader among the young people of Japan. His hate for the Americans ebbed away. He had begun to know victory within his own life and person.

The telex machine stopped chattering out its story and went silent. Tomlinson tore the paper off and made for the exit. The haze of smoke eddied a little as he closed the door behind him, then steadied. In the wire room the two companions remained motionless.

45

Back at his desk Tomlinson sat and read thoughtfully through his story again.

After the morning conference on Wednesday, Ken Lovett compared notes with his feature writers. "Today's thing on airport security shaped up pretty well," he reflected, "though we might have to lose it by the last edition – they're expecting a verdict in that big shares fraud court case, and if it comes through we'll have to slip in that background feature that the City office have written for us. However . . ." he smiled suddenly, "what have you got for me?"

"Did you get my thing about Polycarp yesterday?" asked Miles Drury.

"Polly who?" exclaimed Oliver.

"Just a piece of Miles' efficient research," explained Lovett, "I think we've probably got enough of the early historical stuff now. The bulk of the feature ought to be up-to-date material."

"That's my cue then," said Bob Tipperton. "I've had this from the copy takers this morning already." He held up a bundle of carbons.

"Any good?" challenged Lovett.

"Not bad. Authentic anyway. People who've been going round in circles before they found an answer." Bob selected a sheet and summarized its contents "Like this fellow Phil Townsend – in his twenties now. Kicked over the traces, experimented with marijuana, went on LSD trips, met up with devotees of Krishna – found that too shallow and stumbled on until he saw *The Gospel according to St Matthew* in a cinema at Easter in 1972. That started the ball rolling in a Christian direction. Today he says 'If I honestly look at what Christ did for me on the cross, I can only be filled with a desire to respond'. Bob looked up. That was reported from a lunch-hour church service in Manchester. Is that the sort of thing?"

"I've got a few like that," said Oliver. "Of course some of them are pretty well known for their Christian views now," he went on. "Here's the star of *The Desert Rat* and *Those Magnificent Men in their Flying Machines* – you know, James Fox. He was getting all involved with drugs and whatnot until he had breakfast in a hotel in Blackpool with someone called Bernie, who wrote Bible verses down for him on the paper serviette, and said he was "'spending a day with the Lord'". I've got a quote from James Fox: "'I began to see how the life and death and resurrection of Christ must be true. This fellow could spend a day with the Lord, because Christ had risen from the dead.'"

"Wasn't it James Fox who starred with Julie Andrews in *Thoroughly Modern Millie*?" asked Miles idly.

"That's the one," agreed Oliver. "I've got a few more stories of well-known Christians here – Wimbledon Champion Stan Smith, Olympic gold medallist Kip Keino, Cliff Richard of course . . ."

"Look," interrupted Lovett suddenly. "We don't want too many big names in this feature. This has got to be very, very human, Oliver. We've got to go for the little people, ordinary simple people around the world who find that Easter means everything to them – right now in the seventies." Lovett turned to the features chief sub-editor. "I want you to give all this a fairly strong display when we lay out the pages. It'll be a two-page spread and let's give it lots of impact. A seventy-two-point head and plenty of pictures – the picture desk's getting the last of them processed now." He picked up his brief-case and left.

At five-thirty, Lovett was back at Fleet Street. He had been out all afternoon at a conference, and came in tired and stale. He took a cup of tea over to his desk. On it lay the proofs of Thursday's feature. The headline stared up at him boldly, *The Church that refused to lie down*. Lovett picked up the proofs and read them critically. No doubt about it, the sub had done his stuff all right. And . . . there was a certain cohesion about the whole thing. This story about one Mahomet, for instance – he came from the Maldive Islands in the Indian Ocean, the first islander ever to become a Christian, evidently. Now he was a student in London, unable to return home because his family had disowned him, and his life was endangered. And yet maintaining that in spite of the insecurity and uncertainties, he was given strength to persevere and manage because of the victory and living presence of Jesus Christ.

The cup of tea was cooling rapidly, untasted, as Lovett read on. Here was a paragraph about a deputy headmaster, a cynical agnostic until 1970, when a colleague had brought him to a "guest night" at the local church. Evidently what had grabbed him there was not simply the preaching, nor even the interview conducted during the service, in which an accountant spoke of his faith. It was that *"I could sense that everybody in that church was united by a common link, and was supporting the man at the front as he spoke. It was something I had never encountered before. Christ was there in that place."*

That was it, Lovett reflected. Mary Swan, Mitsuo

Fuchida, Hazel Aylward, Phil Townsend, Mahomet and the rest. None of them seemed to be spiritual muscle-men, or claimed to be anything more than very ordinary people. But for them all, the secret of their lives seemed to lie in a life lived nearly two thousand years ago. And not a very long life at that, mused Lovett. Thirty-three years was it? Thirty years of which were spent in a carpenter's shop. Which meant that you had to boil down the important part to a mere three years. But then, thought Lovett, glancing over the feature page again, what all these people laid stress on was the death and resurrection of this man. So it all really hinged on three days basically.

The words of James Fox floated into focus before Lovett's eyes. *"This fellow could spend a day with the Lord, because Christ had risen from the dead."* There were two things about this really, thought Lovett. These people thought of Christ as literally alive from the grave, and therefore able to give them his friend-ship. But they also saw him as their . . . Champion, was that it? Their representative. The cross and resurrec-tion spell out game, set and match to the carpenter, and consequently every Tom, Dick and Harry who becomes a Christian has a stake in his victory. Even when life proves an uphill struggle, thought Lovett, as he returned to the story of Hazel Aylward and her cancer. Nothing, not even death could stand in their way.

His eyes fell on the story of Dave Mann. Bob Tipper-ton must have found this one, thought Lovett. Another quite ordinary individual, living in Brentwood with his parents, sister and two brothers. Was invited by his friend Neil Hunt to join the nearby church youth fellowship. A lively character. Went to Bible studies, joined in youth holidays and activities, and emerged over the months as a thoughtful Christian. He went to Keele University, which was where the accident took place. For in December 1973 Dave was run over by a bus. Desperately ill, he was taken to hospital. His family gathered around him, with Linda, his girlfriend. After about six days in hospital Dave knew he wasn't going to survive. He asked for his fourteen-year-old brother Jonathan, and gave him instructions for the future. "You've got a skiing party booked up for the holidays," he told him. "You're to go on it. Don't come to my funeral. But you can be thinking of me."

Dave had died on Christmas Eve, untroubled and at peace. His own attitude somehow communicated itself to the two hundred friends who came to his funeral. Especially to his parents, George and Marie who found a new dimension of faith in the whole experience. No one could pretend that Dave's death was anything but a tragedy. But equally certain, it could never signify a full stop . . .

Lovett came to an end. From the inner recesses of his mind a wistful thought broke surface: *I wish it were true.* He brushed it away swiftly; wishes weren't the stuff of which journalism is made.

"Hullo, Ken, they expect the verdict in the court case tomorrow."

Lovett looked up into the face of the editor.

"Court case?"

"The shares fraud. We thought we might get your background feature into today's late edition, but it looks certain for tomorrow now. You've nothing too urgent in tomorrow's leader page have you?"

Lovett looked down at the proof in his hand. "We've done pretty well with this spread on the churches and Easter."

"Pity. You'll have to drop that early on in the day. The other thing's bound to take over."

"Any chance of finding room for a cut-down version of the Easter feature?" asked Lovett.

"Not by the look of things. There's a lot happening and space is tight. You'll have to kill it."

"Right you are," said Lovett. He took a sip of tea from the cup on his desk. It was stone cold.

\*   \*   \*

. . . The Weir public house slipped by on our left. "Nearly there," said Shelagh, and changing down, she eased the car into a side turning marked "Weir Industrial Estate". I turned to Robert Backhouse.

"Well, what do you think? Something like that?"

"That's the kind of thing," agreed Robert. "Mind you the actual stories have got to be genuine."

The car came to a halt.

"They all are," I said. "Every one of them."

# 5

## THE MORNING AFTER

"Your green card please," said the Swedish official politely. It was seven-thirty in the morning and I had just driven my car off the boat at Gottenberg. I smiled at the man in uniform and handed him my passport. He smiled back.

"I see that is your passport," he conceded pleasantly, "but I need to see your green card."

"I've just handed in my landing card at the previous barrier," I parried.

"So? But now I must see your green card."

I dug around among my documents and came up with a receipt form from Swedish Lloyd. At least the printing was in green. "How about that?"

"Yes, yes," said the official, still smiling, *but I want to see your green card.*

The queue of cars off the ship was at a standstill behind me. I flipped through my papers, my Swedish currency and my boat ticket. There was nothing green to be seen. I swallowed hard.

"I'm afraid I have no green card," I faltered miserably.

"But I have to see your green card," persisted the affable Swede.

"Well I haven't got one" – flatly. Brazenly I looked him in the eye.

"I understand. Will you please switch off your engine, leave your car and come with me?"

So this was it, I thought. I was reminded of countless games of Monopoly I had played in the past. *Go to jail. Move directly to jail. Do not pass Go. Do not collect two hundred pounds.* The queue of cars behind me was diverted through another exit, each driver smugly clutching his shiny green card. But not me. I was now the Man Without a Green Card. In a small rectangular office I was asked to part with a hundred and forty Swedish crowns. I had no idea what that represented, but it sounded like a fortune. And even then I got no green card. They let me go with a paltry blue one.

Finally released, I drove shakily off. In Sweden they drive on the wrong side of the road, my friends had told me. At least I knew that. I practised a little around the docks, and then made for the centre of the city. Roundabouts would prove my downfall, I knew – I'd never be able to trust myself on a Swedish roundabout. I drove cautiously. The road seemed excessively crowded even at that early hour. Saabs and Volvos roared past each side of me. Suddenly I noticed a nice empty space and eagerly made for it, only to find myself moments later surprisingly detached from the general melée. Then it dawned on me. I had done what could only be expected of the mere holder of a blue card. I was careering along a tram route!

That's life. Just when you think you've successfully arrived you get pinched at the barrier. Doing pretty well at last, and then you have to go and get dumped. All very annoying and humbling too.

It really isn't at all surprising for someone newly launched into Christian discipleship to encounter a whole new set of problems. Spiritually speaking, he's in a new country altogether, having transferred from "the dominion of darkness" into the kingdom where Christ's banner flies.[1] There are many encouragements of course. Unlike my Swedish experience, everyone, but everyone, has a green card! All Christians are on an equal level, each the possessor of forgiveness and eternal life, each having the privilege of membership in God's kingdom, each indwelt by Christ's unseen Spirit. The greatest problems of all are a thing of the past.

Even so, some people's problems seem to begin when they first declare themselves Christians. A young man may lose his girlfriend for a start. Members of his family may take it out on him, resentful of the strange outside influence now threatening their security. Former friends may give him the heave-ho. And always there is the consciousness of being watched. With appropriate niggling comments:

"Such language, Jim! I'll have to tell the Vicar about you."

"I'm surprised at you, I must say. I thought you were supposed to be a Christian."

[1] Colossians 1: 13.

"I'm off to the pub – that is if Your Lordship doesn't mind."

In the early days of discipleship there is sometimes the uncomfortable sensation of dwelling in no-man's-land. It's the transition period – from driving on the left-hand side over to the right. There's a Book to get acquainted with too – but if you start off on the wrong foot and begin at Leviticus or Lamentations, it may seem to contain concepts and ideas with apparently as much relevance as the Book of Useful Foreign Phrases with its inevitable "My postillion has been struck by lightning". Lamentations can come later – it has its right place and value in God's Book – but a beginner should get straight into Mark's Gospel, and take it in big chunks at a time, preferably in *Today's English Version* or a similar reliable modern translation. After all, a new Christian wants to soak up all he can about the deeds, sayings, and life of Jesus. Just to read about this wonderful Person is enough to dispel the doubt and despair that assail us so often. Having read Mark, I'd go on to Luke next, the human "compassionate" Gospel. Then Matthew and John. John is the deep mystical Gospel. You can go on plumbing its depths, and there will always be more to discover. But this is true of all the Bible, which is why Christians love to read and re-read it. Here is a Book with basically one message – that of re-demption – a rescue story centring in a single Person.

Living as a Christian is not unlike the development of a marriage relationship. When the honeymoon is over there is a good deal of adjusting to be done, new habits to be formed and corners to be knocked off, and it could well emerge that:

*The eyes that over coffee looked so very sweet*
*May not look so tender over Shredded Wheat!*

Are we to infer then that marriage and Christianity prove to be one big disillusionment? Not a bit. It's simply that there is more to them both than a mere initial transaction or decision. As far as the Christian life is concerned, such disappointment as there may be is not because of Christ, but because of one's own lamentable rate of progress.

"I'm going to run a bonfire night for our youth club," said Jack Filby to me one day. He and I were ministering in neighbouring churches in south-east London at the time. "But," said Jack, "it's going to be by invitation only, just for the 'goodies' – it'll be too dangerous otherwise." I knew what he meant, having already met some of the knife-carrying characters who frequented his club. A few days later I asked Jack how the bonfire night had gone. "Could have gone better, Richard, could have gone better," he replied. "The trouble is knowing what to do when you've got bad goodies!"

*Bad goodies* – it's a fairly apt description of the Christian, who is, after all, called to follow the most perfect Being that has ever walked on earth. But his very pilgrimage begins with the acknowledgement of his own need of forgiveness. It continues with an unceasing battle for Christ-likeness of character, a battle that will not be over until the believer finally reaches heaven. Not until then is his "salvation" complete.

"*. . . And so we have those three 'tenses' of salvation,*" concluded the speaker at a students' January conference

I once attended. "I *have been* saved, initially, from the *penalty* of sin by a *Crucified Saviour*."

The sound of ballpoint pens scribbling frantically on paper was almost deafening as the points of the talk were elaborately made and noted down. A student myself, I was hearing them for the first time.

—"Next," continued the erudite gentleman, "I *am being* saved, progressively, from the *power* of sin by a *Living Saviour*. This goes on all my life."

I banged the information into my notebook, and looked up for the next point.

"And thirdly," I heard, "I *shall be* saved, finally, from the *presence* of sin altogether by a *Coming Saviour*. This occurs when I die, or when Christ returns to earth – whichever happens first."[1]

I put down my pen with a feeling of achievement. Another valuable lesson had been learnt, and one which was to stand me in good stead later on as the pressures and battles of Christian discipleship mounted up. For in the time of battle – or discouragement – what helps as much as anything else is a strong grasp of biblical fundamentals. Not that I realized it at the time.

"When you're at a low spiritual ebb, what pulls you through is your doctrine," I once heard said at the famous Keswick Convention held annually in the north of England.

"Well, that's a load of rhubarb for a start," a friend and I complacently agreed afterwards. "What pulls you through is the Lord!"

[1] Broadly speaking the three "tenses" of salvation are equivalent to the three biblical doctrines of Justification (Romans 5: 1), Sanctification (1 Thessalonians 4: 3), and Glorification (Romans 8: 30).

Which only showed how much we had to learn. True, it is the Lord who strengthens his followers in times of setback, but it is only as a man takes hold of Christ's *promises* that he begins to get strong and to "share the divine nature".[1] A good grasp of biblical principles is essential for a clear picture of what is promised and available to the Christian. And of what is not!

For there is a degree of tension built into the life of discipleship that will be with a believer until his dying day. The Christian has begun his journey to heaven, and his possession of eternal life is assured. It says so![2] Equally certain, he has not arrived yet, and he is far from perfect. There is a tension here. It's the biblical tension between the start of the race and the goal, between immaturity and perfection. Unless a believer understands that he is going to have to live with this tension, he can do himself harm. He may fall into despair, imagining that it would be better to give up the battle for holiness, better to abandon any pretence of discipleship, or better at least to opt for a less ambitious brand of Christianity; settle for the Mini rather than the Jag. I can only say to those who have fallen into the pit of depression: Paul made no rash extravagant claims. In later life he describes himself as the chief of sinners. He speaks of discipleship as a battle and a race. The "normal" Christian life involves a whole deal of tension!

But another form of despair is that which regards all tensions as an indication that something went wrong

[1] 2 Peter 1: 4.
[2] I John 5: 11-12.

in the initial turning to Christ. The believer looks wistfully for some new dimension, maybe a fresh and dramatic spiritual crisis that can lift him up and away from his problems. He may feel impelled at an evangelistic service to make some new outward commitment, perhaps for the third, fourth or fifth time. He is looking for something which will remove the tensions. His feelings, which are so fallible and variable, have become his guidelines, instead of God's firm promises of acceptance of him through Christ. To be sure, dissatisfaction with one's rate of advance is a healthy thing. And crises there may well be, some exhilarating, others involving very painful lessons that have to be learnt. Nevertheless, spiritual progress can never be charted simply on the emotion graph. An attack of the blues on Monday morning should never be confused with spiritual backsliding or a loss of one's faith. The presence of tension in Christian living, far from being a bad sign, is a strong indication that progress is being made! The man who is in danger is the man who senses no tension, no problems at all.

I've heard this over and over again from younger Christian friends – "My conscience has been bothering me terribly since I began with Christ; I fail in so many areas that I wonder if I can be a Christian at all." To be quite honest, my spirits rise when I hear statements like this. For they tell me that here is a person whose conscience has been awakened, and who has joined battle! He's conscious of a new adversary, of the discomfort of swimming upstream against the current. The world, the flesh and the devil are suddenly taking a special interest in him. As Brownlow North, a lay evangelist of the last century once put it – "as long as a man lets God alone, the devil will let him alone!"

So what do you do? Be real. Be yourself. Don't even think about trying to copy those smiling Seven Star characters round at the church or fellowship group. That way leads to bondage and frustration. We are to model ourselves on Jesus Christ alone. The wonder of the Christian faith is that when people do just this, instead of developing as dull stereotyped personalities stamped out through a machine, each is gloriously set free to be, uniquely, himself. Himself, and yet, strangely not the man he used to be.

John Newton, formerly a godless slave trader, was to become one of England's greatest hymn writers. He once wrote: "I am not what I ought to be; I am not what I wish to be; I am not what I hope to be; but by the grace of God I am not what I was." Take a second look at those words of New Testament experience. Every one of them screams the truth!

# 6

## THE WILL TO WIN

"Well, if you ask me, it's mighty hard being a Christian," said Andy Stowe cautiously. With a sigh of relief he sat back in his chair again, and fixed his eyes unseeingly on the Bible that lay open upon his lap. There, he'd done it. At last he'd opened his mouth at the Christian Union Bible study, held every week in the College of Education. A mission had been organized only that term by the Christian Union, and Andy – now in the last year of his teacher training – had been converted. At least he thought he had. He had certainly asked Christ to enter his life, and had promptly turned up at the Christian Union. But that had been six weeks ago, and now . . . was it his imagination, or had he lost something of his earlier elation? Anyway, this was a step forward. He'd spoken up at the Bible study.

### Double Think

Suddenly he was aware that silence had descended upon the little group. He raised his eyes. Trevor

Hanning, the leader of the Bible study, was looking at him expectantly. For heaven's sake, he wanted him to say something more!

"It's this sin business," groped Andy uncertainly. "It's all very well being forgiven when you become a Christian. That's once and for all, isn't it? At least that's what the missioner fellow said. Like having a bath all over, he said, and then little sort of daily washes. Right?"

"Right enough," agreed Trevor.

"Well, then," pursued Andy, "I get hung up on these little daily washes! I'm always having to do it. You know. 'Please forgive me for this, that and the other. Sorry I've done that again.' You know. How long does this go on for?"

"It's the devil," explained Julie Preston solemnly. Like Andy, she was in her last year, but had joined the Christian Union eighteen months back. Now she leant forward, her eyes meeting Andy's through the curtain of fair hair that fell across her face.

"It's the devil," she repeated. "It's he who makes us sin. He's been the problem right from the beginning."

"I see," said Andy thoughtfully. "So when I trip up, he's the one to blame then?"

"Steady on," interrupted Trevor, sensing trouble. "It's a bit deeper than that."

"It's the old nature, isn't it?" asserted a confident voice from the other side of the room. Chris Stubbs had spoken up, a likeable bearded individual with horn-rimmed glasses. A small shiny badge glinted on his lapel.

"Old nature?" inquired Andy, wrinkling his forehead.

"Yeah, old nature. Before you were a Christian there was the old Andy Stowe, that used to swear and tell lies, right?"

"Right."

"Well, now there's the new Andy Stowe that wants to follow Jesus, correct?"

"Uh-huh."

"So you have these two natures," continued Chris Stubbs. The old nature that wants to do wrong, and the new nature that wants to live like Jesus."

"And so what do I do when I'm tempted to sin?" Andy wanted to know.

"What do you do? Well . . ."

There was a shuffle in the Bible study. No one, it seemed, quite knew what was the right thing to do. Finally Chris spoke up again.

"You've got to keep the new nature on top," he explained. "I saw this demonstrated once at a Christian camp with a matchbox. The new nature is the smooth top of the matchbox. And when temptation comes along – that's the match – and strikes on the box, nothing happens! But if you let the rough sides of the box get uppermost – that's the old nature, get the idea? – then when temptation comes along – whoomf! – you're in dead trouble."

"But practically speaking, what do I have to do?" persisted Andy.

"Well, you've got to keep that old nature down. When it says to you 'Come on now, Andy, blow your top and say what you like to that so-and-so Chris Stubbs', you tell it to go away."

"But that's schizophrenic," objected Andy, "I can't

63

tell *myself* to go away! It means that instead of blaming the devil for my sins – which is what Julie suggested – I should now blame my 'old nature'. But surely it was the real *me* that wanted to sin, and not somebody else!"

"Okay, okay," said Chris soothingly. "But it's in the Bible anyway."

"Is it?"

"Romans 6," said Chris, turning the pages expertly. "Here it is. Verse eleven. 'So look upon your old sinful nature as dead and unresponsive to sin, and—'"

"Is it dead?" asked Andy in some surprise. "I thought it was egging me on to do wrong."

"You've got to *treat* it as dead," Trevor pointed out earnestly.

"But is it dead, or isn't it?"

"It is dead," said Chris. "Verse 8 has the phrase 'your old sin-loving nature died with Christ'. And so verse 11 says 'So look upon your old sinful nature as dead and unresponsive to sin'. If you don't treat it as dead it'll pop up again," he explained.

"But this is incredible double-think," burst out Andy, "even if the Bible does say it. Ah, I've got the place now." He frowned down at his Bible. "Just a minute," he went on, "my Bible has nothing about 'old sinful nature' in Romans 6. It uses other phrases. For instance in verse 8 it says '*we* have died with Christ', not an 'old sin-loving nature'."

"Yeah, I know," said Trevor, "we're using the *Living Bible* version. It's a paraphrase rather than an accurate translation. It's very helpful," he added hastily.

"Well it may be helpful in other places," conceded

Andy, "But I feel in a proper muddle now. And all because I wanted to know what to do about temptation."

"I'll tell you what to do about temptation," said Julie Preston suddenly. She had been listening to the last few minutes of the Bible study and had felt somewhat out of her depth. "At least I'll tell you what *I* do. I send Jesus to the door."

"Do you?" inquired Andy doubtfully. "How do you do that?"

"I rely on him," said Julie sincerely. "I know how weak I am, and I let him fight my battles for me."

"So what do you actually do yourself when it comes to getting rid of bad habits and things?" asked Andy directly.

"What do I do? Well, I *pray* . . ." Julie began defensively.

"It's all right, Julie, I'm not gunning for you," broke in Andy. "It's just that according to your way there's still another person to blame when things go wrong and you don't get victory."

"I don't blame God," interjected Julie quickly.

"No, but if it's God who's supposed to do all the fighting for us, then presumably when we fail it's logically *his* fault for not giving us the power to win through, and then we have to engage in a bit of double-think."

"Time for coffee," said Trevor. "I'm afraid I haven't led this very well."

"It's my fault," countered Andy. "After all these weeks of silence, I've suddenly found my voice at last!"

They prayed briefly and put the kettle on to boil.

## Trouble-Think

Andy Stowe was never quite sure how he came to be attending the conference. He had left the college, and had just finished his first term's teaching in a large comprehensive school in the Midlands. Someone had passed him a brochure for a Christian conference that was taking place during the school holidays. Although none of his friends appeared to recognize a single name on the conference Council of Reference, and the organization itself seemed a trifle vague in its connections, Andy felt in need of some spiritual refreshment, and duly booked himself a place . . .

A vast chandelier hung from the centre of the conference hall. Andy found that by closing one eye and moving his head slightly to one side, and then the other, he could catch a wide assortment of brilliant colours; a dazzling red, a green, blue, and back to red again. But the opening session had begun, and Andy was forced to take his eyes off the chandelier and transfer them to the speaker.

He was a medium-built man, middle-aged, but with a youthful personality that belied his years, and Andy found himself compelled to listen. The talk was on the subject of the wedding feast at Cana of Galilee, where Jesus changed the water into wine.

"And don't you see the inner meaning of this story!" the speaker was emphasizing. "Perhaps there's someone here who has come to this conference for one purpose only. You've come so that the anaemic, colourless water of your defeated Christian experience can be changed into something very different – the rich and overflowing Wine of God. Isn't that why you've come?"

He's right enough, thought Andy, even if the interpretation put on the Bible passage seemed – well, a bit
forced. It had been a difficult first term at the school,
sorely trying to patience and temper alike, and Andy was
less than satisfied with his rate of spiritual progress. If
only he'd been less tired in the mornings, his prayer life
could have been more disciplined. And if only his
colleagues had been a little more amenable, he wouldn't
have become so irritable of late. As it was, he seemed to
be the only Christian in the staff room. If only his faith
could be of a sort that didn't stir up inconvenience and
trouble, he sighed. The stabbing words of the speaker
arrested him once more, and Andy took out his notebook to make some jottings.

"Why be satisfied with water when you could have
wine?" challenged the orator. "Let me ask you on this
first conference evening, can you honestly say that at
this moment you are completely and totally surrendered
to God? Victorious at every point in your Christian
living? *And if not, why not?*"

Andy was impressed – and flattened at the same time.
He stole an unobtrusive glance at the faces around him,
transfixed in attention. A moment of doubt assailed
him. *I can't be a Christian at all*, he decided. *Not in
front of this lot*. Talk about a failure!

He kept to himself for the bulk of the conference,
dispirited and somewhat ill at ease in the conviviality of
the proceedings. He would perch himself at the back of
the main conference meetings, with his notebook open,
and glean what comments he could as they fell easily,
confidently from the speaker's lips. This Christian life –
it sounded marvellous, incredible . . . unattainable.

67

And he, with his own failure rate, could he legitimately call himself a part of all this? He felt accused and crushed. Wistfully he looked towards the platform again. It isn't double-think that's my problem, he thought wryly, remembering his college days. *It's a kind of trouble-think.* Why can't I be like some of these other Christians . . . ?

On Sunday afternoon, Andy Stowe sat listening to the last of the conference talks. His notebook open, he idly flipped over its pages to check back on what he had previously taken down from the speaker. "Can you say that you are completely and totally surrendered to God?" he read, dispiritedly. "Victorious at every point?" He looked up. A thought occurred to him: *Could the speaker say it?* Could anyone actually *say* that they'd "got there"? Andy fumbled with his Bible, searching for a passage he dimly recalled reading in one of Paul's letters. Here it was Philippians 3: 12:

> Now that I have already obtained this or am already perfect, but I press on to make it my own . . . Brethren, I do not consider that I have made it my own; but one thing I do . . . I press on towards the goal . . .

Well, if the great Paul could say that . . .

He turned his attention back to the speaker. There was no doubting his sincerity. But . . . maybe there wasn't all that amount of substance in what he was saying, after all . . .

Andy transferred his gaze to the chandelier in the centre of the room. He shut one eye and shifted his head; caught a brilliant gleam of green, blue, red, and green again. The green was best, he decided. And – that reassuring Philippians 3 : 12. That alone had been worth coming for, he reflected . . .

## Bubble-Think

Andy Stowe stabbed moodily with his fork at a springy lump of grey matter on his plate, and transferred it to his mouth. That was the worst of leaving home and getting digs, he told himself. No one could make scrambled egg like his mother, of course, but this stuff was . . . well, it was reminiscent of his boyhood days at scout camp. He swallowed some coffee. Lukewarm again.

Anyway you couldn't have everything, he comforted himself. At least here he was in Christian lodgings. Well, that was if you ruled out Mr Prentice of course. His host was sitting in the easy chair by the window, his breakfast completed. A slight man with iron grey hair, he was tranquilly smoking a cigarette as he scanned the headlines of the *Daily Mail* before leaving for the bank.

Mrs Prentice put her head round the living-room door. "You'll have to make do for yourselves tonight, by the way," she announced. "I'll be going to the mission hall this evening."

"Weren't you there only last night?" inquired her husband, raising his head from the paper.

"Alfred dear, they've got a *week* of meetings there," explained Mrs Prentice firmly. "They're asking everyone to come along as many nights as possible. I've got to be there anyway," she continued, "because I'm in charge of the catering."

Andy's eyes met those of his host. Hastily he averted his gaze. "That's all right," he said hurriedly, "we can manage all right if you leave something out for us."

His landlady put a cardboard carton on the table. "Chocolate spread," she explained. "Sorry there's no marmalade for your toast, but what with all these meetings there's just been no time for any shopping, and . . . well, we have to put the Lord's work first, don't we?"

Mr Prentice drew heavily on his cigarette.

"If there's one thing I'm always telling him," confided Mrs Prentice to Andy, "it's that we could all do with a bit less worldliness and a bit more consecration. We were only hearing last night—"

The door closed quietly. Mr Prentice had taken his paper and left for work.

"I said we were only hearing last night," resumed Mrs Prentice, as she swept up the coffee cups, "that we could all do with a bit more consecration. *Power* was the word the man used. We ought to be more like the Christians in the Acts of the Apostles."

"Isn't that why the power of the Spirit's given to help us?" remarked Andy.

"Then where is it?" challenged Mrs Prentice. "*Where is it?* In fact that's what the man was saying. He said—" she screwed up her face in an effort of recollection – "'If you had the power of the Spirit in your life, why aren't you like the Christians of old? Why aren't you victorious at every point in your living?'"

I've heard this before somewhere, thought Andy, but he said nothing.

"Christians ought always to be on top," pursued Mrs

Prentice. "If I miss the bus, I ought to be able to praise God for it!"

Or burn the toast, thought Andy, but again he said nothing.

"Anyway," said his landlady, "I must be off and get the food for the meeting tonight. There's just one thing—" she paused.

"Yes?" said Andy.

"We're going to be moving in nine months' time. The Lord has led me to start up a Christian guest-house on the south coast. Alfred will be giving up his job."

"Really? What'll he be doing then?"

"Well, we're not worrying; we're just waiting on the Lord to provide in his good time . . . The only thing is . . . what with the expenses of the move and everything, could I ask you to pay a little more for your weekly rent?"

Andy saw the red light. "The fact is, Mrs Prentice, I may not be here much longer myself. I'll gladly pay extra for the next few weeks, but in a month's time I'll be moving myself."

"But . . . this is very sudden. Why do you want to move? What with the fellowship here and everything?"

Andy looked thoughtfully across the breakfast table. "Maybe the Lord told me to move," he said quietly . . .

\* \* \*

"I'm not at all sold on your friend's illustration of the matchbox with two sides or 'natures' to it," said Alan Cartwright.

It was Bank Holiday Monday, and Andy Stowe had

seized the opportunity of the church outing for an un-hurried talk with his minister, as they sat together at the front of the coach. "It's just that I've got a few loose threads that need pulling together," Andy had pleaded.

Now he looked at Alan Cartwright. "The matchbox idea didn't really grab me at the time," he admitted. "You see, there was Chris Stubbs in the CU Bible study telling me – from the *Living Bible*, mind – that my old sinful nature *was* dead – but that I had to keep remembering to *reckon* that it was dead in order to stop it popping up and having a go at me! I'd have gone potty if I'd started thinking schizophrenically like that!"

Alan nodded. "I love some of these modern para-phrase Bibles, Andy," he acknowledged, "and the *Living Bible* is really great. It makes the whole thing come alive in a remarkable way – but it's dangerous to rely on some of these versions at every point for an accurate translation from the Greek New Testament."

He paused. "Man, of course, is one nature, not two. A fallen, sinful nature, desperately needing forgiveness and renewal. Which, of course, God gives through Christ in the Gospel." He smiled. "And that came to you in the mission."

"Right enough," agreed Andy. "But now that I'm a new Andy Stowe," he continued, "possessing forgive-ness and new desires and allegiances, what *is* meant by the bits in Romans 6 that refer to '*our old self*' being dead? Because it has that in the Revised Standard Version," he added earnestly.

"Exactly," said Alan. "I think where your friend went wrong is that Romans 6 has more to do with

72

Christian beginnings than with progress and victory. Surely 'our old self' means exactly what it says – the old Andy Stowe before he was a believer. You've said goodbye to him now, haven't you?"

"You mean that my pre-Christian life is a thing of the past?"

"Yes. It's dead and finished. You no longer stand under the condemnation of sin. Christ has taken the penalty of your sin upon the cross, and in that sense has 'died to sin'. But because you're related to Christ, *you* therefore have died to sin. The old set of factors no longer holds true. Your old life is a distant phase now. It's dead."

"So when I read that I must consider myself dead to sin," persisted Andy. "I'm not trying to screw myself up to believe something that's not true."

"Of course not," retorted Alan. "It simply means that you acknowledge that when you began with Christ you were turning your back on your old life. It belongs to the past. From that point on you began to grow into the new life – renewed as you were by the Holy Spirit."

"Explain this a bit more," urged Andy.

"All right. Can you remember when Britain's currency went decimal? A new set of factors had come into being. The old system no longer applied. It was dead. And, of course, we all had to start *thinking* decimal. There was no point in going back to the earlier phase. Not that it's *impossible* to think back in terms of pounds, shillings and pence, and every now and then I catch myself doing it even today, but certainly it's completely illogical and unnecessary for us to do so. See the point?"

Andy thought he did.

"It's not impossible to slip back into the old realm from which you came," continued Alan, "but as you're now in the new realm under a new Master – *and* with the power of Christ's Spirit to help you – it would be illogical to do so."

The coach had now drawn up outside a café, and Alan and Andy got out for a stretch and a cup of coffee. When they were seated, Andy resumed his questioning.

"The trouble is, Alan, that I find that the pull of sin is as strong as ever – in fact if anything more so than before."

"I'm very glad to hear you say that."

"You are?"

"Certainly. You're in good company with Paul! If you read the last twelve verses of Romans 7, you'll see his description of his own experience as an advanced believer – it's one of fierce wrestling against sin in his life. The fact that you feel this pressure too is a pretty strong indication that you're making progress as a Christian and that the Holy Spirit is at work strengthening you in the battle."

"Really?"

"Of course. Sin didn't really bother you before that mission, did it? The person who ought to feel worried is the one who feels no pressure and no battle. In all likelihood he isn't even a Christian yet."

"That's not what I thought at the time of the mission," grinned Andy over his coffee cup. "I thought I was going to be set free from all my problems!"

"You *were* set free from the main problem," Alan replied. "You were taken out of one realm and transferred to another. But far from being freed from the fight, in point of fact you were set free *for* the fight. Until you began with Christ you couldn't even fight!"

"It *is* me doing the fighting, is it?" queried Andy. "I remember a girl in our CU saying that when she was tempted to sin, she 'sent Jesus to the door'."

"It would be more accurate to think of Christ sending *us* to the door," came the answer, "but, of course, he sends us to fight equipped and renewed by the Holy Spirit. Philippians 2 puts it beautifully – 'Keep on working, with fear and trembling, to complete your salvation, *for God is always at work in you* to make you willing and able to obey his own purpose'. The power comes from God, but we are required to co-operate."

"Let's get back to the coach," suggested Andy. "I've got another question for you that's been bothering me for a long time." They finished their coffee and made for the door.

"Well let's have it then," said Alan, as the coach pulled out on to the road again. "Your question?"

"It's this. No one seems to be able to answer my question 'What do I *do* when I'm tempted?'"

"That's where we all want help, Andy," said his companion soberly. "The simple answer, if you want it in a word, is 'You choose not to sin'."

"Oh. Don't you have to ask for special power to be able—"

"Why do you want to ask for power? Isn't it there?"

"Ah," said Andy, "I've just remembered what a landlady of mine once said when I told her that we have the power of the spirit to help us. She said '*Then where is it?* Why aren't you experiencing victory? Where is this power?' What do you say to that, Alan?"

"Well, just as a start, let's hope that *she* was living a consistent victorious life in her own life and home, if she was going to ask that question," came the quiet answer.

Andy suddenly looked out of the window.

"And secondly," went on Alan, "the question she asked was the wrong question." He paused.

"God doesn't mock us, you know." Alan's voice was very quiet now, and Andy had to strain to hear his words above the noise of the coach engine. "He doesn't pick us out of the realm of darkness and then leave us like a kitten mewing on a piece of wreckage in the sea, waiting and hoping for something miraculous to turn up. Far from it. Pentecost was given us. To the whole Church of God, that is. And every Christian, however new, is given the equipment of the Holy Spirit's power from the outset. He wouldn't be a Christian otherwise. Romans 8: 9 tells us 'Any one who does not have the Spirit of Christ does not belong to him'. You memorize Colossians 2: 10 some day, Andy."

"Which says—?"

"Which says, 'You have come to fullness of life in him'."

"You mean, fullness of life in the relationship with Christ?"

"That's it. In other words the equipment, the power, is there from the beginning in the Holy Spirit. That doesn't mean we don't face a lot of battles, and sometimes crises. And every now and then a sudden spurt forward! But the question your landlady asked was the wrong one. *It isn't a battle about power, but a battle of the will.* Now if she had asked, 'Where is the *desire* for victory and Christ-likeness in the Christian Church today?' she would have been on a more profitable tack."

"So that our problem is one of—"

"Disobedience, and the lack of desire to win," Alan finished.

"You're saying we can win if we're *willing* for victory?"

"That's right. You can test yourself out on this. So often we moan that we don't have victory, but when it comes to the crunch, we're not prepared to co-operate with God, to face the uncomfortable inconvenience of saying 'no' to our sins which are so dear to us."

"And we really can say no?" wondered Andy.

"We're commanded to do so. So many of the New Testament commands urge us into active obedience. We're told to *run the race*, to *resist* the devil, to *fight*, to *wrestle*. The battle is ours. When we sin, it isn't a mythical former sinful nature that makes us do so. It isn't even the devil who can make us sin. We're out of his kingdom when we belong to Christ. He can do no more than tempt us. No. When we sin, it is because we have chosen to sin, and for no other reason."

"So there really is no special secret formula about victory?" concluded Andy.

"Well, that seems to have emerged in your first – what, eight months of discipleship, Andy? There are no short cuts to holiness. There is no special élite of super-Christians. And there is no secret technique for victory beyond feeding our souls and strengthening our wills to obey the mind of our Master. How's that for a three-point sermon?"

"I like it," said Andy.

# 7

# THE SILLY SEASON

In March of 1974 the news media around the world splashed the story of a new fad that had its beginnings in some of the campuses of the United States – that of "streaking", or running nude from A to B through a crowd of onlookers. For this kind of activity an audience is vital. It only needed a few TV cameras to appear, and within a week the craze had spread right across the American campus scene, and further beyond too.

The silly season is nothing new. It tends to hit Britain round about August, when summer is high, the holidays are on, when newsmen are scraping the barrel for something of interest, in short, when activity is at a low ebb and everyone is thoroughly bored. It also seems to be a pattern of life that from time to time our society welcomes any little excuse for a break in the steady plod that makes up so much of our living. This is equally true of the Christian scene.

*"Delegates are strictly prohibited from the fixing of stickers to the camp coffee cups."* I remember hearing the

rather bizarre notice being given during a national Christian conference on evangelism that was held a few years ago at a holiday camp in the north of England. It was at the height of the "sticker" craze, and some of the younger conference delegates were driving the camp waitresses mad with frustration by their earnest attempts to evangelize them through the little soap-defying slogans that clung, limpet-like to the camp crockery with their message, "*Smile, God loves you!*" A superficial approach the stickers may have represented, at least they were an indication of some joyful enthusiasm around the place even if they were no more than a passing fad.

Me, I welcome anything that can add a touch of joy, brightness or originality to Christian work and worship, particularly if it's well done. Cartoon-drawn visual aid figures executed in fluorescent colours, audio-visual techniques, modern church furnishings, concealed lighting, palm trees in the foyer, carpets on the floor, murals, microphones, what-have-you – we could do with more of that. Better that than gaunt, freezing buildings in which indigestible jargon-strewn pulpit fare is sometimes served up as "helpful solid teaching". Or where the barest of church furnishings confront you in areas where most homes have central heating and wall-to-wall carpeting. By all means, let's splash money on the overseas missionary cause, but let's abandon the hypocrisy of spending money on our own homes while palming off the Church Centre with the throw-out carpets and chairs – leaving it for months on end with the rubbish, sellotape and Christmas decoration remnants still cluttering its neglected undecorated premises.

Attending to needs like this can hardly be called gimmickry; it's simply a matter of straight commonsense priorities.

At the same time, *pure animal excitement* must come under the category of "bonus", when applied to Christian discipleship. For we were never promised such by the Founder of our faith. "Happenings", jamborees, special efforts, thrills and excitements have a place, but only a limited place on the Christian landscape. Ninety per cent of our horizon is composed of rough terrain, where discipline, "stick-ability" and a tenacious grasp of the essentials are at a premium.

Very often, the first real test of a Christian's endurance qualities occurs about two years after his launching – that is, assuming that there was a discernible turning-point, which is not always the case. Frequently then, the painful lesson has to be learnt, that while flying is exciting, walking is more important! If the immature beginner has been taught to rely upon a diet of fizz, gimmicks and spiritual thrills, then the possibility exists that he may be added to the company of ecclesiastical gypsies who hot-foot their way around the circuit of available churches, tasting here and sampling there, but generally unsatisfied anywhere. Reason? The honeymoon period of faith is over. A superficial grasp of Christian basics has given rise to the delusion that there is nothing more to learn now. A hunt begins for some fresh diversion in the attempt to break new ground.

An American writer, Henry Frost, describes a stage of his spiritual life in which he was getting absorbed in minor novelties. He writes, "*I had reached the point where my interest was centering in what I may call the* '*curiosities*' *of the Scriptures.*"[1] Now such an experience is understandably common to many Christians. This is the period of discipleship that frequently sorts out the men from the boys. It is an interesting, but entirely scriptural phenomenon, that whenever a church or an individual believer has taken a major step forward, it has been due, not to the discovery of a new doctrine, but to a deeper understanding of the old fundamentals. This has been so in every major revival of the Christian faith in our history. At the centre of the sixteenth-century reformation was the re-discovered doctrine of justification – the truth that a man or woman is accepted by God, entirely in virtue of the atoning death of Jesus upon the cross. Come to the Evangelical revival of the eighteenth century, and a glance at the great hymns emerging from that time show where the centre of the revival lay: *When I Survey the wondrous cross, Not all the blood of beasts, There is a fountain filled with blood, Jesus thy robe of righteousness, Victim Divine, And can it be, There is a green hill,* and so on.

All worth noting, in view of the perfectly understandable desire in many Christian circles for something "new" – particularly where spiritual life has ebbed and apathy has set in. The message of history is, "Come back to the old paths and tread them again." Or, as a preacher in a sermon on Depression put it, "Remember in the Darkness what you learnt in the light". The temptation often is to do the opposite, to shelve the familiar and to cast around in desperation for something novel, for some new formula that might

[1] Henry W. Frost, *Miraculous Healing*, Marshall, Morgan and Scott.

miraculously lift the depression and bring a new surge of power and life.

Maybe this is partly why some Christians talk today with enthusiasm about "the second blessing", a line of teaching that emphasizes the need for a special experience of the Holy Spirit subsequent to conversion, often termed: "the baptism in the Holy Spirit". Scripture, of course, prompts every Christian to long for more of God, and yet, interestingly, once Pentecost had taken place, we never find the biblical writers urging believers to seek or wait for such a "baptism". *Their emphasis, rather, is on what has happened.* Not that the Christian life is a static affair. The great emphasis of Paul's letters to his young converts is on living out, and growing into, what they already have and possess. But, only once in his letters does he mention the idea of being baptized in the Spirit, and there we read, *"For in one Spirit we were all baptized into one body"* (1 Corinthians 12: 13). From which I learn that the baptism in the Holy Spirit is viewed as having taken place in the past, as far as believers are concerned, that it is the common experience of all Christian people, initiating them into the "one body" of Christ and his Church, and that therefore it is the uniting bond between everyone who belongs to Jesus. A positive and thrilling truth indeed! Young believers ought not to be thrown, therefore, when they are asked by sincere and well-meaning fellow-Christians, "Have you received the baptism in the Holy Spirit?" It is, perhaps, a bad reflection on the standard of pulpit teaching today that we *should* be puzzled by such a question. For according to the New Testament, the newest, rawest

Christian is qualified to reply, "Yes, I belong to Jesus Christ, and as such have been baptized in the Holy Spirit." We should be careful, however, never to pour cold water upon another Christian's experience or apparent "second blessing". The believer may well be in for a number of high water-mark encounters in the course of his pilgrimage. But we would be wise not to construct from such experiences a doctrine that is to be insisted upon for all believers.

I was interviewing Festo Kivengere, the world-travelled revival leader from East Africa upon this very point, during a public meeting. He had flown in from the Far East, where he had been conferring with the leaders of the great revival movement in Indonesia. Shortly before that he had been called in by the revival leaders in the Solomon Islands, where an unprecedented work of the Holy Spirit had been taking place, and thousands had turned to Christ. And now he was in England, on his way through to Switzerland, and then back to Uganda. "What about this 'second blessing'?" I asked Festo.

"I don't speak about a second blessing," he replied. "No. In Africa if you speak like that in the revival areas they will look at you with amazement. The Holy Spirit comes and pours himself upon you when you receive the Lord Jesus." And in reply to my question, "What is the greatest need of Christ's Church across the world?" Festo replied unhesitatingly, "It is to catch a fresh vision of the Person and work of our Lord and Saviour. In other words, the centrality of the glorified Christ. What we fear is that when the cross is not in the centre, things go wild. God's balance is the cross."

It was no surprise to hear this testimony from Festo Kivengere. I had read something similar in a letter from another revival leader from Africa – Heshbon Mwangi of Kenya. Reviewing some fourteen years of growth in the Church in East Africa, he commented that not a year went by without some subtle attempt being made to divert this movement of the Spirit from its central message of the cross.

"The evil one came as an angel of light," wrote Heshbon Mwangi of one year, "bringing visions of the cross and of the Lord to one and another of the more earnest ones, *making them pin their faith to these outward and visible physical manifestations instead of trusting only in the precious blood of the Lamb.*" Of another year he writes, "Satan worked in this way, that when they met for fellowship, they spoke much of dreams and visions, and had controversies about such things as the eating of pork . . ." Elsewhere he comments, "Satan deceived people into listening in passivity for the guiding of the Holy Spirit. By this means people were deceived into listening to evil spirits."

Yet again he writes, "This year Satan caused the preachers to weep when they were preaching, and so caused weeping in the gatherings. People thought they had been saved by these signs of emotion. They even made restitutions, returning stolen things, but they were not delivered from sin. *Emotion is not salvation.* Satan also produced lying prophecies; e.g., that the Europeans would be put out of their shambas (landed property) and that these would be given to the saved; many lapsed when these prophecies were not fulfilled."

Of another year, Heshbon states, "Satan came in

84

another way, i.e. telling people that because they had not spoken in tongues they were not filled with the Spirit. Some waited in vain for this, others were given supernatural manifestations. Divisions were formed. Brethren, if a man is saved, let him throw away doubt, and let him not think the working of miracles is important. There is nothing greater than to have the Lord Jesus in us . . ."

The devil has a number of ploys available when it comes to distracting the Christian from the basic fundamentals and from the path of discipleship. I love the Old Testament story of Nehemiah's rebuilding of Jerusalem's shattered walls, following the Jews' return home from exile in the sixth century BC. It took every ounce of Nehemiah's strength of mind to resist the distracting devices utilized by a certain Horonite, a snake by the name of Sanballat. First he tried to *discourage* God's worker by derision, pure and simple. Next he tried to *divert* him from the task in hand by inviting him away for a conference! To which Nehemiah sends reply, "I am doing a great work and I cannot come down. Why should the work stop while I leave it and come down to you?" Undeterred, Sanballat next tried to *exhaust* the determined builder, by bombarding him with repeated invitations. And, meeting with no response, he lastly tried the angle of the direct *threat*. All to no avail, because, in the words of Nehemiah, "the people had a mind to work".

If the devil – and he is a foe of real personality, as Jesus taught clearly – cannot make inroads by one method, he will unfailingly experiment with another, switching over with the skill and speed of an experienced tactician. For years, Christians in the West have been vulnerable to the soft approach that lulls its opponent with carefully selected soporifics. Materialism is one such powerful drug. A relatively comfortable life, coupled with the absence of any real physical persecution – and there you have it, the steady, insidious erosion of all motive, purpose and dynamic. An easy life with a bit of church-going, a show of Bible-reading, a respectable tip in the plate – result: ineffectiveness, or, at the least, a blunted cutting edge.

Naturally, if a believer cannot be tempted to ease up, then he may be persuaded to *freeze* up – with the help of a few deftly arranged shafts of persecution. Or mere discouragement for that matter. There comes a stage with many a Christian, when he senses that at last he has victory over a besetting sin. Then, maybe months later the biblical truth slowly dawns upon him that it was, after all, *only a victory that he had to go on winning*. Just discourage him enough, only divert him from the true goal of Christ-likeness, once get him to settle for less than a hundred per cent – and mentally he's already a backslider!

*Or perhaps he can be made to seize up.* Here's the other extreme. It's the devil in a clerical collar, turning up at the church – urging one and all to greater and yet greater efforts at zeal and holy living – fostering a "meeting-itis" life-style of Christianity, the Christianity of the flashing eye – jutting jaw – fixed smile variety. Alas, there are all too few natural expressions of joyful Christianity in the West – but once let such expressions become *manufactured*, and the last state can be as bad as the first. "Hullo – someone jumping with the joy of the

Lord over there? Then let's all jump. *Keep* jumping! Higher . . . and higher!" And over the top.

A little far-fetched? Perhaps. But the following story – which would horrify every section of Christian opinion – was told to me personally in March 1974, and helps to illustrate the point – and provide a warning. Liz (I am going to call her that) was a glorious down-to-earth Londoner, and a member of our church. She had been invited to a "revival meeting" in her area, and happily enough she went along. During the evening it was customary for people to be invited by the leader to come forward for hands to be laid on them for healing. In many cases the laying on of hands was accompanied by the collapse of the person concerned, and a "body-catcher" was generally on hand to assist. On this occasion Liz was among those who went forward. "I thought it would help my asthma," she explained. However, when the leader's hands were laid on her, she could feel herself being dragged down. "I could feel my body about to collapse," she put it later. "All my earlier experience of the Holy Spirit had lifted me up and given me peace and strength to cope with the situation. But this was a frightening experience in this church. And inside I felt, 'No, no, this isn't from the Holy Spirit.' And I could hear the man saying to me, 'Now come along, give yourself up to the Lord.' But I knew I'd got to get away from the force of this. I staggered away, and got back to my seat. I felt so terrible. I couldn't talk to anyone about it."

But the real parting of the ways for Liz came, when a friend of hers had gone forward for healing. "She'd been several times already over the weeks," Liz recollected. "Sometimes she seemed a little better, maybe, and then she'd slip back again. On this particular night she went forward again, and then the leader at the front proclaimed it to the whole church as a miracle." Liz accosted the "body-catching" assistant at the close. "I said to him, 'Don't you think; it's not glorifying to the Lord to have a thing like this happening. *You* don't think it's a miracle, and nor do we! And yet you're allowing it to go before the whole congregation as a miracle.'" He then said, "I know it wasn't a miracle. And you know it's not a miracle. But there are people at the front of the church who want to see a miracle. And there are some people at the back of the church who've come a long way tonight, and *they* want to see a miracle."

"That was the end for me," said Liz simply. "Apparently we weren't to make it look wrong, because they had to be satisfied that they were going to have their miracle. At the expense of my friend! So I left. And I was told afterwards that the leader there had prayed a little prayer *'for those who have gone out angry tonight!'*"

Let me repeat – I cannot think of a single leader from any branch of Christianity who would have given such an occurrence his approval. And yet this happened within the precincts of a main-line denominational church. Experiences like this are not unique either. The tragedy is that such incidents can all too easily cause Christians to over-react in the opposite direction – against all that *is* spontaneously Spirit-given and genuinely biblical. The lack of teaching in the churches of today has left many of us Christians wide open to any and every movement that sets itself up as "biblical", and let's face it – I have yet to meet the devotee of any pseudo-Christian movement who wasn't convinced that his beliefs were anything but "balanced"! The current craze for exciting experiences, at the expense of living the life of faith and trust, comes as a partial result of decades of a joyless, frigid church establishment. However it means that no church member of today can be insulated against literature, meetings and proselytizers of every brand. We're out in the open now. That's no bad thing either. It will ultimately make for a purified church. But perhaps "The Silly Season" is a misnomer for the confused religious scene that confronts us today. Os Guinness puts it well, "If it is twice as easy for a Christian to speak into such a situation, it is also twice as hard to speak into it intelligibly. Faith that is faddish can be as dangerous as faith that is false."[1]

The Christian life is a long-distance affair, hence the warning note sounded in this chapter. Effort, study, discipline and active battle are required from the believer as he co-operates with the power of God's indwelling Spirit. There are times when he fails, when he disobeys, or when he is lured on to some slip-road that diverts him from his true course. What to do in such circumstances? First, be grateful if you have enough discernment to see that you *are* off course. Secondly, don't lie down on the ground signalling dismally for the ambulance! Get up, ask for forgiveness and go on. Thirdly, learn a lesson from your experience, and determine that the same thing won't happen again. And lastly, if you really have gone down a blind alley and don't seem to be getting anywhere, try and get back

[1] Os Guinness, *The Dust of Death*, IVP, p. 54.

to the place where you went in, or find an older Christian friend who can help you to that spot.

There's an old English folk song that runs wistfully:

> And it's – *Oh, the Briary Bush*
> *That pricks my heart so sore;*
> *And if once I get out of the Briary Bush,*
> *I'll never go in any more!*

# 8

## ALL ONE HAPPY FAMILY

"Say I like this idea of a cooked breakfast," rumbled Hal Burnaby, chewing appreciatively on a mouthful of egg and bacon. He waved his fork in his host's direction. "Quite a change from the waffles and syrup I was raised on."

Neil Miller wrinkled his nose. "You could only be an American, Hal," he murmured. "Waffles at breakfast time!" He slit open a letter, and unfolded its contents as he sipped his coffee. "Letter from a church member Betty!" he warned, glancing at his wife across the cornflakes packet. "It's from Sybil. Let's hope the— Oh!" he broke off, and then scanned the letter more closely. "Listen to her first sentence," he resumed. "'Dear Reverend Miller . . . I am saying this in love—'"

"Oh dear," interrupted Betty.

"Count-down for a rocket," grinned Hal Burnaby.

But Neil Miller's face was set in an anxious frown as he read the letter silently through. He had had the charge of this, his first church as a minister, for three years now, and while his ministry in general was appreciated by the bulk of the congregation, the "honeymoon" period of his ministry was well and truly over.

He lifted his face from the letter. "It's on the same tack as the other letters, Betty," he said wearily. "Threatening to leave the church if I go on choosing twentieth-century hymn tunes for the Sunday services."

"Not that he does choose all that many," put in Betty. "There was only one in yesterday morning's service. But that, it seems, was one too many for Sybil, if she's now threatening to leave."

"And good riddance too I'd say," commented Hal, helping himself to the marmalade.

"Oh no, Hal," Neil interjected quickly. "You don't understand. Sybil's been a member of this church for decades. She's elected as a leader almost automatically at every annual church meeting. We simply couldn't lose her because of a few new hymn tunes."

"But if she's like that, she's not a leader worth having," objected the American. "What she's saying in effect is 'Do things my way or else . . .' That's no way for a mature, democratically elected Christian leader to behave."

"Well, at least we're better off than that church in the Midlands," rejoined Neil. "Do you remember, Betty? I read it in the *Daily Telegraph* a few years ago. 'Choir resigns over Rector's lively hymns' was the headline."

"What, the whole caboosh?" Hal wondered.

"I've got the article here," Betty chimed in. "I cut it out and kept it in my bureau." She pulled out and unfolded the crumpled yellowing press clipping. "Here we are," she said, "*Daily Telegraph*, tenth of February 1971". She looked up at her husband. "That's right," she confirmed, "the organist and ten members of the choir resigned after refusing to agree to 'brighter and more lively hymns'. And," Betty continued, "it seems that the resignations ended a seven-month 'work to rule', during which the choir stood silent and the organist clasped his hands on his lap every time one of the Rector's modern numbers was announced . . . what's the matter, Hal?"

But Hal Burnaby could make no reply. He had slumped forward on to the kitchen table, his hands over his face, convulsed with helpless laughter. "Oh you wonderful English!" he finally gasped, when he had recovered himself. "And you mean to say that this made the national press?"

His hosts assured him that it had.

"Big deal!" boomed Hal. "And all this, not even over the words, or the doctrine of the hymns – just the tunes?"

"If you want it exactly," said Betty precisely, "in the twelve months preceding the bust-up, the choir had sung four hundred and forty-one traditional hymn tunes and sixty traditional anthems. They had been asked to sing a total of seven modern hymns, but had refused."

There was a resounding crash in the little kitchen. Hal Burnaby had fallen off his chair. He was still gurgling insanely as he was brushed down and helped back to his place again.

"You wonderful English!" he repeated, shaking with mirth. "Here you are, the Church with its back to the

93

wall, congregations thinning out, the world exploding around you, Northern Ireland on your doorstep, militant communism hammering at the gates; your Commonwealth gone, your oil at the bottom of the North Sea; your churches closing by force of economics alone! And with the house on fire around your ears, what do we find you doing? Re-arranging the furniture inside! Resigning over hymn tunes that haven't reached the age of a hundred!"

"But Hal, what am I to do about this letter now it's been written?" pleaded Neil.

"File it, son," came the prompt reply. "I know a minister who keeps a file marked 'Complaints and Grumbles'. And if a member of the church family hasn't the decency to bring any queries to him personally but starts resorting to cold impersonal letters, why, he gives them the same treatment, and consigns their precious document to a nice safe impersonal file – preserved intact for all posterity!"

"Neil, you'll have to go and see Sybil," remarked Betty quietly.

"You'll do nothing of the sort," retorted Hal. "She can wait till the fellowship meeting, or next Sunday morning's service. But as for me," he continued, "I'm going to get myself a nice invitation to tea with Sybil during the week. I just can't wait to find out what makes an Englishwoman like her tick. She's either got a unique sense of humour, or she's some kind of an oddball!"

"Don't book her up on Saturday evening," warned Neil. "The young people's group are having a barbecue then, and they've asked you to come as their special guest from across the water!"

"It'll be my pleasure," smiled Hal.

*    *    *

"This bit of meat's not done yet," said Hal Burnaby. He prodded tentatively. "And this one's still mooing! Be another ten minutes yet." He wiped his hands on his trousers.

"How are you enjoying yourself at the Millers, Hal?" asked a voice from the circle round the barbecue. The American looked up from his work at the questioner, a dark-haired youth in his first year at university, who went by the name of "Python" to all and sundry. Hal had gathered that his real name was Monty.

"I'm having a swell time," he replied warmly. "And you? How do you like having Neil Miller lead your church?"

"Well, it's not bad," said Python doubtfully. "Though I don't know that you could really call it a church for young people."

"Python's right," a girl in the group nodded vigorously. She had earlier introduced herself as Mandy, a self-possessed sixth former and a Bible class leader at the church. Now she looked at Hal with troubled eyes. "The services are *deadly*," she sighed. "It's not that Neil Miller doesn't preach okay – he's fine, and he understands us. It's just all the . . . well . . ."

"Trappings," finished Python. "You know. The old language. The dirges. And the clothes! I'd feel ashamed to bring my friends to a church service, when that lot at the front are all trigged up like simpering angels."

"I came to church the other Sunday with my mate from the printers," put in Mick, a spectacled individual with a droop moustache and wearing frayed denim jeans that Hal observed were composed almost entirely of multi-coloured patches. "You know what happened?" he continued. "My mate was so nervous of coming that he togged up a bit for once. He didn't say anything to me about it, but I could see, he'd got on his Afghan coat and all. And then blow me down if an old duffer in a pin-stripe suit didn't come up to him and say, 'Look here lad' – Mick altered his voice in a passable imitation – 'Look here lad, you're always welcome here, but don't you realize this is the house of God? Next time you come on a Sunday, why not come wearing your best?' My mate didn't know what to say," recollected Mick. "He *was* wearing his best, and nervous as a kitten too! Naturally he didn't come again. We just sat at the back, and when they'd finished grinding through the service, he was off."

"You had a problem there," Hal acquiesced. "I guess you folk always sit at the back, right?"

"Well we do," agreed Python, "largely because it's not our scene, you see. Everything's wrong – the gear, the language, the singing. It's not that we want to sing rubbish," he added hastily, "but there is some more up to date stuff now, with words that everybody can understand and—"

"I heard of a sort of house church the other day," interrupted Mick. "Quite a lot of young people are going along to it. They've mostly left their own churches and they go along to this place. They usually take turns leading, and they reckon this is better. One of them asked me to go along next Sunday, I thought maybe I'd give it a try."

"Kind of do-it-yourself gag?" inquired Hal.

"That's it," said Python. "They've asked me along too."

"Have you been a real Christian for long, Python?" Hal wanted to know.

"About two years. It was at one of Neil Miller's first guest nights that I accepted Jesus Christ for myself."

"My, you must be mighty grateful to Neil Miller for that guest night," smiled the American.

"Of course. I've always—" Python broke off in mid-sentence. "Oh I know what you're going to say Hal," he resumed. "You're going to say that I ought to show more loyalty to the place where I began my Christian life. I know, I know. But it's *hard* . . ." his voice trailed away.

Hal Burnaby turned his attention to the barbecue. "We're doing pretty well down here," he commented. "Who'd like some of this stuff?" The discussion was abandoned for a while as the twenty or thirty present got down to the business of the evening.

Hal handed Mandy a fork. "You do this kind of thing often?" he asked.

"Not often," said Mandy, biting into a roll. "Not with meat the price it is in England. But sometimes we go off to a Chinese restaurant on a Saturday night. And I'm always ready for a Wimpy Bar. I love Wimpies," she added. She looked up at Hal. "To come back to what we were talking about a moment ago, I agree with you, Hal, about loyalty and all that."

"But I never said anything—"

"No, I know. But the others could see what you felt.

97

I'm quite happy to go on at the church – especially as the teaching's always from the Bible. If it wasn't, then I might feel differently."

Hal nodded.

"This is the secret of our group really," Mandy continued. "The Lord's at the centre, rather than social activities. I can think of youth fellowships that never take off because God quite obviously *isn't* at the centre. He's just dragged in at the end as a sort of . . . well, Epilogue, I suppose."

Hal nodded again.

"But this is different," Mandy went on. "Bible study is the big thing. And, of course, there's always the church behind us. We can go to Neil or one of the other leaders if we need help, and we're always getting the Sunday by Sunday teaching. Even if the rest of the service is deadly!"

"Another reason, maybe, for not leaving the church and joining this other group," commented Hal, lowering a piece of onion into his mouth. "You bright young things need the depth and teaching that Bible stalwarts like Neil Miller can give you. Especially when you're young," he added. "The danger with the little groups that split off is that all too often they *are* just an escape bolt-hole, with not enough leadership, not enough depth and not enough experience to keep going. After a while the members begin to shrivel. Or they fall out with each other, and start forming a new clique. Fragmentation is quite a problem in church life over in the States too."

"I get so cross with Mick, Python and the others," said Mandy indignantly. "They just don't seem to see this. But then I get so cross with Neil Miller too for not juicing things up in the church a bit faster! I lead the girls' Bible class, and it's just heartbreaking to see them fall away once they're invited into the dreary traditional services."

"No use getting cross with Neil Miller," said Hal thoughtfully. "You've got to help him."

"Too right," said Mick who had suddenly joined the discussion. "I once heard a convention speaker tell everyone to go straight back and dig out their ministers and say 'I just wanted to come and tell you that I love you, pastor!'"

Mandy laughed outright. "If I told Neil that, I think he'd suspect me of something! Betty would anyway."

"No pastor needs to be told if his people love him," reflected Hal. "If they love him, they'll show it in a hundred different ways."

"Such as?" queried Python, who had drifted into the circle.

"Well . . . sitting up at the front of the church?"

There was an outraged chorus. "What?"

"And bringing Bibles and taking notes on the sermon?" suggested Hal, unperturbed.

Mandy laughed again. "That got you, didn't it?" she chided. "But I think Hal's absolutely right. It would encourage Neil, wouldn't it?" she looked at the American for confirmation.

"Too right, it would. And it would improve the preaching still more if he saw you all taking notes on what he was saying!"

"We'd be right up against the toffs at the front if we did that," countered Mick dubiously.

"And they'd be up against you little lot!" grunted Hal. "But after all, they're your brothers and sisters in Christ. What does the family of God mean if we can't be close to each other and mix up a bit at worship? And at other times?"

Python spoke up. "I heard the leader of one of the Jesus communes say that it was no use trying to bring the two generations together now," he challenged. "That it was best to let the oldies go on their way, with their creaking monolithic institution, and to let the new generation of Christians tread their own path, with house churches, Bible cells and everything. That the two generations could never come together now."

"Defeatist talk," said Hal shortly.

"Defeatist?"

"Sure. Once you admit that Christians can't bridge the generation gap, you're admitting that Jesus Christ isn't big enough to hold us together! Either he *is* big enough, or else all the talk about his world-wide international family is just a lot of empty baloney."

"You've got a point there, Hal," admitted Python. "Maybe I'll hang on at poor old plodding Mother Church, and just hope that it'll change one day."

"I guess you can even improve on that," prompted Hal quickly. "I figure that if you lot threw your weight into the church and prove that they could rely on you for your service, your worship, your weekly offering in the collection . . ."

"And sat at the front with a Bible and took notes," added Mandy.

"Like the lady says," affirmed Hal, "sat at the front *and* sang those dirges till you were blue in the face – then several interesting things might happen."

"Like . . . ?" prompted Mike.

"Well, for a start Neil Miller would love you for it. Secondly, some of those old people, who regard you just as that proud immature lot who sit at the back with folded arms, would sit up a whole lot. And thirdly, people like you, Python, would sooner or later get elected as a leader in the church. And then think of what you could do!"

"Sounds as though it's worth sinking one's energies into a church like ours after all," declared Mandy.

"Like the lady says," agreed Hal once again, "too many Christians these days are like the joker who said he wanted to join the navy, but firmly refused to be attached to any particular ship!"

*     *     *

A complaint was being lodged during the bi-monthly council meeting in the church hall. Vociferously too, Hal Burnaby decided, as he gazed thoughtfully at the speaker's face, aflame with indignation. The recently held Sundy evening youth service was the subject in question and Hal, an invited guest at the meeting, was agog with curiosity. He took a pencil and picking up his agenda sheet, tore off a small corner. On it he scrawled, *Is this Sybil?* and passed the small scrap of paper casually to Neil Miller who was sitting immediately on his right. Neil glanced down, took the pencil, and ticked an affirmative against the question. Hal recovered the paper, screwed it up and dropped it into his pocket. He then turned his attention back to the speaker.

Sybil was in full flight. "The tail's been wagging the

dog in this church a little too long!" she expostulated hotly. "In my day there were no such things as 'youth services' every two months. We young people were expected to take our place in the regular adult worship of the church the moment we were too old for the Sunday School. We certainly didn't expect to be *entertained*!" – the last word was flung out into the room with an explosive flourish.

You're quite a girl, Sybil, thought Hal to himself. A force to be reckoned with – and some! He sensed Neil recoiling beside him under the weight of Sybil's on- slaught. She was still speaking. "*And*, Mr Chairman, I therefore formally move that this council reduce the number of youth services during the year from six to one!" She sat down, quivering.

There was a silence. Neil coughed nervously. And now what, thought Hal. A little opening, dear Lord, he silently breathed, let someone give me a teeny little . . .

A chair scraped noisily on the floor. Hal looked up. A gentleman had stood up to speak, middle to late age, very English, wearing a pin-stripe suit. This must be the guy who got under Mick's skin, Hal decided. He listened, fascinated, to the precise faultless English. The real goods it was, there was no mistaking it when you heard it.

"I think, Mr Chairman, that we've been through all this before," the speaker was saying, in measured tones. "We all know one another fairly well, and I doubt whether there are many angles left for us to explore as regards this issue. It just occurred to me that our guest from the United States . . . er, Mr . . . ?"

"Burnaby," supplied Hal politely.

"Thank you – that Mr Burnaby might be able to enlighten us a little from his experience of church life in America, before we come to a decision tonight."

The gentleman in pin-stripe sat down carefully. Every eye turned towards Hal. Neil Miller raised his eyebrows encouragingly. "Mr Burnaby?" he invited.

"Thank you," Hal obliged. He took a deep breath. "We certainly have youth services in American churches," he emphasized, "plenty of them, and many churches find them valuable." He paused. "But if you want my own opinion, you could do worse than follow the advice of the lady who spoke a moment ago." He nodded across towards Sybil. "That is, virtually close down the youth services." He smiled reassuringly at Neil who had stiffened visibly. "These youth services have evidently been part of a very healthy phase in your church life," continued Hal. "If they've done nothing else they've illustrated the immensity of the generation gap and the urgent need for change in our church life and worship." He looked around the room. No one stirred. "But youth services by themselves," went on Hal, "won't bridge the gap. In fact if anything they'll widen it."

Neil spoke, understanding dawning. "You mean there's a danger of creating two clienteles?" he asked, "The youth service crowd every two months, and the more traditional element the rest of the time?"

Hal inclined his head. "Already in the States we have the problem of two churches developing – fast. And I guess you've got it here. That ought not to be."

Sybil was nodding her head with warm approval. "And so you agree that the right approach is to wean these young people away from the youth service approach, and to educate them into the real solid meat of adult church worship?" she demanded.

"Of course," replied Hal. "That is, if you're all satisfied that your worship is relevant to today's generation, that it's adequately geared to the seventies and eighties." He looked around. "Are you?"

"Well . . . *yes*," replied Sybil. "Of course church worship takes a little getting used to naturally . . ."

"Naturally, naturally," murmured Hal. He had whipped out a notebook. "I was trying to figure it out last Sunday during the church service here," he continued, "and discovered that I needed a little educating myself in your English ways of worship!" I'd be mighty grateful if someone here would kindly explain to me a term that was used in one of the opening sentences of the service." He looked down at his notebook. "I have it here. The word 'dissemble'. It was a phrase used in connection with our sins. Your minister exhorted us not to 'dissemble'. What does that word mean please?" Hal looked up with a disarming smile.

"Well, it means what it says," responded Sybil firmly. "It means . . . It means . . . what was the word again?"

"Dissemble," said Hal meekly.

There was a pause in the meeting. The pin-striped gentleman cleared his throat. "I think I've got it," he ventured. "It means to ignore things, doesn't it?"

Hal shook his head apologetically. "I'm sorry, sir. I looked it up in a dictionary after the service, and that wasn't what it said."

"Surely it means to murmur about something?" insisted Sybil.

"Wrong again," said Hal softly, looking sorrowfully down at his shoes.

"Well, come on, Hal. Tell us what it means," exclaimed Neil Miller urgently.

"Me tell you?" Hal looked surprised. "But me, I'm only a backwoodsman from America. I've never even seen that expression before." His eyes suddenly crinkled in a wide grin. "See what I'm getting at?" he asked. "Here you are, the leaders, the cream of the church" – he looked directly at Sybil – "brought up on these phrases all your lives; using them every Sunday, but even *you* don't know what they mean! And if *you* don't," he added, vehemently stabbing the air with his forefinger, "then for crying out loud, how are the rest of the church going to get along with your 'real solid meat of church worship'?"

Silence fell again. "Pardon me, I've talked too much," admitted Hal. "It was kind of you to ask me to your meeting. I'll clam up now."

But now, it seemed, no one wanted the amiable American to retire from the discussion. The debate waxed fast and furious, enthusiasm running high as tongues were loosened, and prejudices abandoned.

"So it's the whole church that needs bringing into the seventies," concluded Neil at last. "That's the idea isn't it, Hal. No more youth services, you think?"

"Stunt services never did any lasting good," came the reply. "They only caused frustration to the young, in that they weren't often enough, and to the old in that they upset the apple cart all too often! If a church is genuinely adapting itself progressively to the culture of its day it won't really need more than the very occasional youth-type service, because the whole family of the church from the top to the bottom will be advancing together in contemporary worship."

"It won't be easy for us older ones," said Sybil wistfully. "Everything of stability in our lives has been taken from us in the last thirty years. Now even the faith itself seems to be in danger."

"Not that," contradicted Hal. "That can never change. And our Lord will never change. He is *the* great stabilizing factor in a changing era. No, the very possession of the Gospel of Christ in our lives impresses upon us the urgency of expressing it just as clearly as we can in today's world."

"So our minister has a sizeable job ahead of him then," conceded the pin-striped gentleman benevolently.

"I don't think so sir, with respect," replied Hal. "If you leave it to Neil to push through every necessary development in the church life and worship, you'll be waiting till Armageddon. It's not a job for one man. It's an attitude that has to stem from the top. From all of you. In fact it would be better for the church as a whole if *you* were all seen to be pushing Neil into action. Once that's established, then the way has opened up for steady development through the church."

The meeting broke up. Sybil approached Hal. "I was meaning to ask you, Hal," she began, and then stopped. "I may call you Hal, may I?"

"Of course."

"I was meaning to ask you," resumed Sybil; "I do so want to have a talk with you about America. Would you care to come and have tea with me next Tuesday?"

"I'd love to," said Hal. "By the way, may I call you Sybil?"

*     *     *

It was a Sunday night three months later. Neil Miller was facing his congregation as he prepared to deliver his sermon. Curious, he thought, how there seemed to be a new buoyancy in the air. What had caused it? A number of intangible factors possibly. He looked around. Of course! The front seats were filled with young people. All armed with Bibles, it seemed. And, good gracious, half of them clutching notebooks! Some of them had taken part in a brief musical item just before the prayer time in the service – a song chosen to tie in with the theme of the evening. There had been a mixture of new and old. Some of the service language was still a trifle Elizabethan, Neil reflected. But . . . that would alter gradually with the passing of the months.

He lifted his head. The congregation was quietly seated now, waiting to listen to Neil's address. He opened his mouth. "I was talking to an American friend yesterday who has just flown back to the States," he began.

A rustle swept imperceptibly through his listeners. Neil's eyes fell on Sybil's face, as she smiled with happy recollection. That was almost the best of it, he thought to himself, as he peered down at his notes. He and Sybil were friends now in the family of Christ. And who was that seated next to Sybil? Neil risked another peep. It was Python.

# 9

## A PIECE OF THE ACTION

"Eddy, what tie am I going to put on with this shirt?" I asked helplessly. A groan answered me as a tousled figure rolled out of the neighbouring bed and felt blindly around on the floor. Eddy Shirras was looking for his spectacles. "I can't help you on a problem like that," he mumbled drowsily, "until I've got my specs on! Just a tick."

There was a further minute's fumbling, and then the pyjama-clad figure of a Christian Fleet Street publisher padded over to my bed in the grey dawn of a September Saturday morning.

Eddy stooped and gazed at my shirt and an assortment of ties lying on the bed. Then, "Have the purple," he finally pronounced. "Just the very one for the winding-up concert in London tonight."

We were sharing a room, Eddy and I, for the last night of the hectic *Psalm Praise* tour, that took us, and a choir of nearly fifty, right around England for a series of nightly "launching" concerts for a new book of psalms published by London's Falcon Press. It was a great concession that we were allowed a bed at all, of course. Eddy had been involved in a motor accident a few weeks back, and I'd had a spell in hospital; hence our privileged role as the invalids of the party. For most of the week it had been all go – up at the crack of dawn, a rushed breakfast and then into the cavernous double deck "National" motorway coach; rehearsals on the road as we travelled, under the tireless direction of Michael Baughen, dynamic leader of the work at All Soul's Church, Langham Place; a non-stop starch diet at innumerable motorway service stations, the concert itself, and then as likely as not, a pile of "dead" curling sandwiches at midnight, and so to bed, with a mysterious invisible disc jockey inside your head, obligingly spinning a succession of *Psalm Praise* numbers as you slid around half the night on slippery nylon sheets!

But the minor adversities were virtually eclipsed by the exhilaration and purpose of the whole enterprise. By the "fun" side of over forty highly diverse personalities thrown together for a week, above all by the sheer quality of fellowship and fulfilment experienced in doing something for God's kingdom.

After a week of travelling, interviews and singing to enthusiastic crowds all over Britain, you finally stagger home feeling like a million dollars. And then quite suddenly it's all over. Wound up and finished. Important tasks are awaiting you. Like paying the newspaper bill, mending the dolls' house, feeding the ginger beer plant. Gradually you come down to earth, pick up the threads of your life again, and wake up to another "normal" day.

For the bread and butter of Christian living is a steady, on-going pilgrimage. That's what Jesus promised us. Once let a man imagine that the average Christian ought to be a kind of spiritual Roger Moore, and he starts getting itchy feet! Begins to think that there is no way in which his nine-to-five job in town can possibly serve the cause of Christ his Master. Or the university student can be conned into dismissing the notion that God's first call on his priority centres in the passing of his exams, rather than in a welter of "spiritual" activities. Again, redundancy is no small problem in the West today, but there are too many Christians needlessly out of work at present, living on the earnings of others in the false belief that a secular job is inconsistent with holy living.[1]

Fear also paralyses activity. It is all too easy to look around at the staggering problems of global dimension on every hand, and to take fright. To imagine that unless we can aspire to service and Christian leadership on a pretty spectacular scale, we stand little chance of making much of a dent in contemporary society. I remember as a child in Kenya seeing a group of missionaries standing on a terrace, vainly trying to beat back a locust swarm. It was a terrifying sight. The sky was literally blacked out by the cloud of millions upon millions of locusts. I recall seeing my father among the men, attempting to protect the nearby crops from the approaching swarm. He was actually swatting in the air with a tennis racket! At the end of the afternoon a mere twenty or thirty slain marauders represented his entire tally.

[1] Ephesians 4: 28; 2 Thessalonians 3: 10.

Today we are dazzled by swarming statistics, dwarfed by towering power structures. One reaction, in the face of such escalating pressures is simply to throw in the towel and give up. An alternative is to *swat* energetically, blindly, in all directions, every Christian for himself, in a frenzied attempt to stem the inexorably advancing foe. A meeting here, a protest march there, a revival get-together yet elsewhere, a tract campaign one day, a blizzard of stickers the next, a crusade, a conference, house meeting, prayer meeting, fellowship meeting, cell meeting. And every one of them vital . . .

I was once talking with Herbert Cragg – from whose powerful ministry I learnt at first hand for five fabulous years in Beckenham. "Here we go again, Richard," he shook his head wryly as he held up yet another urgent request for his endorsement of a certain "pioneer" enterprise. "I'm reminded of that little verse in the psalms – 'They came about me like bees!'" It is not that blind swatting achieves nothing. On the contrary, there will always be a dozen menacing predators within swatting distance, and all waiting to be knocked off. You cannot deal with them all, however and the danger lies there. The whole Christian scene is littered with half-finished projects, once enthusiastically, bombastically hailed by their founders as "an exciting new venture of faith". There is a casualty rate among Christians too. Unco-ordinated witness and activity lead to the over-strain and even collapse of the individual. Paul's twelfth chapter in his letter to the Romans reminds us that what God is looking for in any follower of his is "a living sacrifice" – not a half-dead one!

I have sometimes heard enthusiastic Bible teachers exclaim, "There is no such thing as 'strategy of evangelism' – just get out and talk to people about Jesus." *People?* Which people? Douglas Webster, a leading exponent of Christian mission, has made the comment that Jesus never told us to love *everybody*. In a study on The Good Samaritan,[1] he writes:

> That is not Christian ethics – nor is it practical ethics. Jesus told us to love *somebody* . . . It may not be easy; it is at least definite and concrete. We are not called to love Africa – but to love an African, and through him to love Africa and other Africans.

It certainly seems to be a fact of Christian history that the best and most lasting enterprises began in the realm of the small but specific! Just to look at the New Testament is sufficient demonstration that the churches established by Paul in Asia Minor were founded not on a policy of blanket evangelism, but through humble contacts established with specific individuals, singled out for mention in the apostle's letters. Or look at TEAR fund, the international relief agency established by the Evangelical Alliance in Britain only a few years ago. When George Hoffman took over as director in 1968, he was simply handed one small file! No vast organization was set up, there were few overheads. The fact remains that today it is one of the most sensationally expanding pieces of work on the Christian horizon, based on prayerful planning and the direct involvement of numerous churches and youth groups around the country.

[1] D. Webster, *Who is My Neighbour?* Highway Press.

*"We do it together."* This assuredly is the secret behind any growing work of God and every effective local church. It starts in the realm of praying together. Shelve that as the agreed number one priority for a fellowship's mid-week activities – and integration goes out of the window. You're back to locust-swatting again. In another book, I have mentioned an Indian friend of mine, Vijay Menon, a converted Hindu, a man in ceaseless demand for evangelistic speaking engagements all over Britain. A fascinating thing about Vijay is that he resolutely refuses to absent himself from his own church mid-week prayer meeting. "Apart from Sunday worship," he comments, "the weekly church prayer meeting is the top priority for me. In my diary I block that evening out right through the year. It's automatic."

Let real concerted prayer join hands with the Gospel at the very centre of a Christian community – and a purposeful unity sweeps in to integrate that body and the work it carries out. All jockeyings for position, every angling for "recognition", all efforts to erect mini-empires ("my" missionary meeting, "my" house group) will look as absurd and ridiculous as the disciples squabbling at the last supper over the matter of the top places in the kingdom. And not only so. The man of prayerful loyalty who has one assignment in the fellowship – say, the setting out of the chairs and the arrangement of the room – will attend to it ungrudgingly, will think his job through and apply his imagination to it. So much of Christian work is just that – putting out the chairs, clearing away the rubbish, switching on the heaters, changing the fuses, licking the stamps and paying the expenses. Expenses, by the way, are a case in point when it comes to visiting speakers. Frequently their travelling is not covered at all. Or they are made to feel churlish in accepting anything. Sometimes a book token is proffered in lieu of cash, on the ridiculous assumption, presumably, that the speaker will lean out of his car at the next petrol station and inquire "Do you take book tokens here?" The above-mentioned Vijay Menon was once asked to itemize his expenses at the close of a crowded meeting. He replied thoughtfully, "I have spent some twenty hours preparing this talk for you. I have driven half across England to get here. I have missed my lunch, and I expect to get home again at 2 a.m. You can send me whatever you think best." It is salutory to think that a speaker can go to such endless trouble, when the organizers cannot even give twenty minutes to working out his travelling expenses. On another occasion Vijay was asked "What are your expenses?" To which he grinningly shot back, "A wife and two children!"

To be a front-liner in the service of Christ involves a whole deal of care, discipline, attention to details and hard work. Take Tim Saxton, for example, producer of BBC Radio London's programme *The Orange and Lemon Club*, presented each week by Michael Baughen and myself. Michael and I may be the presenters, but the hard work is largely accomplished behind the scenes by Tim, and some fifty or sixty volunteer radio enthusiasts around the Greater London area. Bible dramas are put together, musical items are recorded and sent in, personalities and places of interest are visited and then featured, and the whole half-hour programme has to be shaped and then edited by Tim. Frequently this means he will be up until 2 or 3 a.m. making as many as two or three hundred edits. All unpaid work, and all done in his "spare time"!

As a matter of fact the front-liner can quite quickly be picked out from the back-liner just by attitude and conversation alone. I once heard Lorne Sanny of the Navigators emphasize this during a visit from America to the Keswick Convention. His talk was a reminder to me of the grumbling and pettiness that plagued Moses and Joshua back in the Old Testament as they led the Israelites. What would a reporter on the Amalekite Battlefront have heard as he probed for information on the latest situation?

"Well, it could be worse," the reply might come. "We've lost a quarter of our men in the last two hours, but we can hold on. Maybe you could ask them to send up a few more arrows and spears from the back – we're running a little low here."

And so to the back line. "How are you getting on?"

"Oh it's terrible. Just terrible. We've run out of melons!"

Another voice chimes in dolefully. "Manna again for breakfast!"

And that's the difference. A Christian's conversation alone is enough to give him away, will accurately pinpoint the strength and measure of his commitment to Christ's cause.

The Christian life is a supernatural thing. It cannot be lived off an individual's own batteries. It is a life of the Spirit in a believer's personality, filling him and using him in ways that he might never have dreamed possible. It is the Christian's exciting privilege to discover and use the gifts and abilities with which the Holy Spirit has endowed him. Every disciple of Christ has at least one gift, for Paul reminds us "To *each* is given the manifestation of the Spirit for the common good" (1 Corinthians 12: 7). And from Peter "As *each* has received a gift, employ it for one another" (1 Peter 4: 10).

I used to think, at university, that what was required was a single dramatic "filling" of the Holy Spirit if one was to be any use as a Christian. It was only later that I learnt a more biblical emphasis, which I now crystallize in three simple statements.

*The life of the Spirit calls for a discovery and use of gifts already given, rather than a wistful longing after others.* The gifts of the Spirit are many and varied. Paul features three lists of gifts in his letters,[1] and all three lists are different from each other! We are not sausages stamped out of a machine. Not all are to have identical abilities and callings. Every disciple has his place, uniquely, in the service of Christ and of his fellows. The term "the charismatic movement" is in use a good deal today – a name derived from the Greek word for "gifts". I do not mind fellow-believers using this term in the least, as long as it is recognized that *every* Christian has at least one gift, and is to use it to strengthen the rest of the church, and that the *whole* church of Jesus Christ across the world is therefore one great "charismatic movement!" But I have a second statement.

*The life of the Spirit calls for a continual and daily "filling", rather than a single crisis experience.* I love the

[1] Romans 12:6–8; 1 Corinthians 12:8–10; Ephesians 4: 11–13.

New English Bible rendering of Ephesians 5: 18 –
"Let the Holy Spirit fill you," because it best captures
the thrust of the Greek verb, which is Present Impera-
tive Passive – if you'll pardon the grammar lesson. It
thus conveys the thought of a continuing, repeatable
experience. While there are bound to be some peak
moments along the road of discipleship, the New
Testament does not encourage us to look for them. As a
Christian opens his life to the resources of Christ's
Spirit in daily prayer and Bible reading, as he repents of
sin in his life and asks for renewed forgiveness, as he
gives himself in daily obedience to Christ's laws and
directives, so he may expect to be filled for service and
usefulness. His character will go through a progressive
transformation as the "fruit" of the Spirit begins to
reveal itself.[1] The mark of a Spirit-filled person,
supremely, is a consistency of Christian life-style, and a
Christ-likeness of character. I have a third statement.

*The life of the Spirit calls for an active obedience, rather
than a passive waiting.* If today, Christ's followers appear to be lacking in power and holy living, it is not
because power is not available; it is because through
disobedience we are grieving the Holy Spirit. The Spirit
is given to every believer – *therefore* we are to obey and
get active! I think it was Jessie Penn-Lewis and Evan
Roberts, leaders in the great Welsh revival, who in one
of their books had a significant paragraph headed, "Why
Waiting Meetings are profitable to evil spirits." They
made the point that Christians should not hold gatherings for the specific purpose of *waiting* for the Holy
Spirit to come and fall on them, as such a procedure is

[1] Galatians 5: 22–23.

an open invitation for evil spirits to come and masquerade in the guise of an angel of light, and so deceive the believers. No. Once Pentecost was past, the "waiting" period was over. Indeed we should not even "wait" for revival, however much we may prayerfully desire it. We are to get on and do something! Frequently, I have found myself, at the end of a piece of Christian service, feeling twice as fresh, twice as fulfilled as before I began. Paradoxically, the way to be filled with the Spirit is to be *emptied*, and to share one's blessings!

All too often, when a Christian is approached for a piece of service – he hedges and hesitates. There is a right way and a wrong way of doing this! It is right when healthy modesty and genuine concern for God's will are the motivating factors behind such hesitation. Sometimes, however, it may rightly be suspected as a cover for the disobedience that runs a mile from commitment and possible inconvenience. Sadly, cynically perhaps, my spirits have sometimes plummeted on hearing the words "I'll pray about it", piously, even glibly trotted off. Inside something tells me, *They're not going to do it*. Different, so different, from the time that a certain Colin Smart was approached for a job! In his early twenties at the time, immensely likeable with shoulder-length hair, he had the authentic genuinely "rough" accent of East London that sent at least one radio drama producer into raves of delight. I offered him the leadership of perhaps the most demanding group in the church – that of a mixed group of early teens. Colin looked at me. And with three words he saddled himself with a week-in, week-out commitment of preparation, organization and sheer hard work for several years ahead. I watched his face as it creased into a smile and "the voice" abrasively replied, "Yer, orl roight!"

It seems that those who have achieved much for God have generally had the simplest of aims. Paul wrote, "One thing I do." Really, Paul! We all thought your hands were full of different enterprises; Paul the historian, Paul the traveller, Paul the apostle, evangelist, pastor and missionary strategist. Oh and tent-maker. But the secret of Paul was his integrated life – his basic Christ-centred aim that underlay and shaped all other ambitions, imparting strength and dynamic to everything he touched.

I once saw Billy Graham on the screen, being interviewed about his hopes for a forthcoming crusade. "And how many converts are you looking for from this campaign, Dr Graham?" came the somewhat cynical question.

I wondered what the reply would be. A brash "Sixty thousand?" Perhaps the modest "Numbers don't really count – it's quality that matters"? Or the pious "Eternity alone will reveal the extent of our efforts"? It was none of that.

"One," replied Billy Graham. "*Just one!* If we could make one real convert here, we feel it would have been worth the trip. If I could win just *you* to Jesus Christ, it would have been worth coming!" It was the perfect answer.

Or there was Ken, a missionary friend of our family's. He was working in a part of Africa with the Church Missionary Society when he was told by the country's authorities that he had twenty-four hours in which to leave the country, to pack up his belongings and go. An able carpenter, he had been about to start on a project of equipping a newly built church with pews. So what did he do? Pack feverishly? Charge around the mission station like a whirling dervish, re-organizing everything in sight? Not a bit. His last twenty-four hours were spent in building *one* pew, so leaving his African colleagues with a model on which they could base *their* labours, and so finish the work. He also left them, of course, with a remarkable model of how a goal-orientated Christian can behave with serenity under pressure.

Here is the safeguard against fragmentary wild-cat schemes that never quite come off, the antidote to the empty exhaustion that stems from a random swatting of the air. It is the steady, purposeful Spirit-filled life that God has planned for each of his agents; the life of one loyalty, the life of one goal.

Perhaps the greatest educationist that East Africa ever had was Carey Francis of Kenya. I remember him from my boyhood days. A tough resilient Christian, he earned the respect of all who passed through his hands at Nairobi's Alliance High School over many years. At his funeral most of the Kenya cabinet members turned out to carry his coffin; hundreds of his African friends gathered round the grave and filled it in with their own hands. He once said this, *"When I go, I want God to find my letters answered, my work up to date, and me hard at it."*

## 10

# THE FINAL SHOWDOWN

"Il n'y a pas de petroleum ici?" I inquired brightly of the Swiss taxi driver. I had just arrived in Geneva for a conference and was trying to polish up my French. At least it was better than the Swahili my mother used to lapse into on earlier continental family holidays! Today the taxi driver simply shrugged and lobbed a salvo of foreign phrases at me over his shoulder, from which I deduced that, yes, there was a problem about oil supplies, but that it wasn't too bad. Yet.

That was in December 1973, only months after a few days fighting in the Middle East had jeopardized the world's energy resources at a stroke. Doubtless we were going to scrape through for the time being, but already in the minds of political and economic commentators, the writing was on the wall. One day, sooner or later, the lights will be switched out – for good. Which is only what the Book of Revelation has been emphasizing all these years. In chapter 18, the end of the world system is prophesied, with the political world in disarry (verses

9–10) the business world facing collapse (verses 11–17), and all maritime trade wound up (verses 17–19). The end is also spelt out for the world of music, technology, food production, human relationships and our energy supplies (verses 21–23). "Never again will the light of a lamp be seen in you . . ." (Today's English Version).

Just how and when all this is to work out is not for us to say. I remember hearing Garth Hewitt satirizing the pessimism of modern man in his song *Good Old Man* that he sang at "Spre-e" – a Billy Graham youth event in London's Earl's Court arena:

> *And they say we'll all be dead in 1990,*
> *Because there'll be no drinking water left at all;*
> *But don't allow that thought to cause you panic,*
> *Because fresh air to breathe runs out the year before!*

Is this how the present world system will close – with a steady running down of the machinery, until all life on the planet is finally snuffed out? Or with the scene of radio-active ruin portrayed in Nevil Shute's *On the Beach*? Or with the permanent hell of George Orwell's *1984*? The Bible tells us otherwise. It speaks in terms of a planned and definite *conclusion*, and there are some voices in contemporary society that are beginning to agree. Arabella Churchill, grand-daughter of Sir Winston Churchill, said in 1971, "My grandfather used the phrase 'The Iron Curtain'. It seems to be that what is facing us all now in the Final Curtain." Or to quote the well-known columnist Bernard Levin, "The final picture that is likely now is portrayed not so much by *1984*, as by the Book of Revelation."

"How otherwise could the Bible end?" asked Fred Mitchell once in some memorable convention Bible studies. "Supposing it had ended at the Epistle of Jude? Then all that we should see would be ungodly men in their ungodly deeds to which they were committed, and the saints committed to, and contending ing for, the faith once for all delivered to them. The issue in such a case might appear to be in doubt; but no, the Bible is complete, for in the last book we see the climax of all the redemptive purposes of God."

The Book of Revelation may not be very easy to understand, but one thing about it is as plain as daylight. Reminder after glorious reminder comes crashing through the pages of this wonderful book to assure Christ's followers that he is the great Winner, and that the devil and his allies are the great losers. Chapter 20 portrays the final battle, culminating in the total defeat of Satan and his whole entourage. The defeat will be but the logical and final outcome of the rout inflicted on the kingdom of darkness at the time of Jesus' death and resurrection. The Book of Revelation hinges upon chapter 12, where Calvary and Christ's victory are seen from the spiritual and angelic standpoint, and where believers are reminded that "they have conquered him (that is, the devil) by the blood of the Lamb". Thus the Christian is not living and working towards victory, but *from* the position of victory already achieved at the cross! The return of Christ is simply the final winning ace. The battle will then be over. Death, suffering and evil will be destroyed, and Christ's followers will then be with him for ever.

Not that at present we are without a battle on our

hands! The truth is that "the devil has come down to you in great wrath, because he knows that his time is short!"[1] Anyone serving Christ on the front line has always known the force of this statement, and not least is this true today. Today we are caught up in a battle of ideologies that traverses the world – a battle in which we face such a churning cake-mix of philosophies that it is very difficult for us to have a balanced picture of the true situation. We're too close to it all for one thing. It is no exaggeration to say, however, that surviving and winning as a Christian is a very much more complex and dangerous matter than it was a decade ago.

"The BBC are here, Kurt. Are you ready to see them?" There came a murmur of protest from the bed in our spare room, and Kurt Koch sat up. Or to be more precise, Dr Kurt Koch, the world-travelled Lutheran pastor from Germany, who was on a ten-day visit to England. "These BBC boys are too late," he rumbled as he got off the bed. "Everywhere it is the same with the people who demand interviews. They arrive late, and then they ask the wrong questions!"

It was no surprise that the BBC wanted to interview Kurt Koch, an internationally acknowledged authority on Christian counselling and the occult, the author of some seventy books, and a visitor to well over a hundred different countries. In the early sixties the subject of the occult was virtually a closed book in the Western world – today it represents a fascinating and highly dangerous area of experimentation and money-spinning profiteering, as films like *Rosemary's Baby* and *The Exorcist* have amply demonstrated.

[1] Revelation 12: 12.

"You can only counsel people in this area if you are under the protection of the blood of Christ," emphasizes Dr Koch, "and only if he has given you the commission and authority for this work. It is very strenuous. I have known people who have tried to do such counselling, and they broke down and had to enter a mental hospital. I warn people not to enter this field of work – particularly young Christians. It is too dangerous."

I remember a contact I once had with a young man. He had been under a form of occult bondage, and went to a minister for help. Unfortunately the minister was a man who had developed a "taste" for exorcism. There are such men today, eager to discover and demolish demons everywhere – demons all too often of their own inventive imagination. They talk of demons of bad temper, laziness, and so on – talk which is indignantly dismissed by Dr Koch as irresponsible and extremist. I have even known of a case where a slide projector was subjected to the laying on of hands in an attempt to free it from its mechanical deficiencies. But to go back to the young man – the outcome of his visit to the minister was that the problem had indeed been removed from him *only to transfer itself to the minister concerned*. If this sounds extremely frightening, it is meant to. The over-confident "professional" approach is as open to attack as the exorcism attempts of the inexperienced amateur. A genuine man of God with a case of occult bondage on his hands will invariably hope that it is his last. It is not that he distrusts the protection that the cross of Jesus affords him, for he is indeed safe – providing he never exposes himself to occult practices. It is simply that he dare not underestimate his enemy.

For the enemy is angry. Has been angry ever since losing the battle of nearly two thousand years ago. Refusing to admit defeat until the final showdown, the Church is made the chief target of his many-sided attacks, and meanwhile time is running out on him. "*Children, it is the last hour*," writes John[1] in his first letter. In point of fact we have been living in the "last hour" ever since Christ's death and resurrection and gift of the Spirit, and it has been largely due to impatience on the part of Bible students that mistaken attempts have been made from time to time to ascertain when the final crunch moment will be.

Leaders of the True Light Church of Christ in North and South Carolina expressed "surprise" and "shock" in January 1971 that the world had not ended in 1970 as had been predicted by their founder, Cunningham Boyle, way back in 1870. The most pressing problem for the church lay now in the finding of new employment for those who had given up their jobs in anticipation of the end. Not that the failure of Mr Boyle as a prophet had adversely affected the church's membership! The last that was reported in the world's press was that many of its members were still expecting "dramatic developments".

It is the "last hour" largely in this sense; that as far as God's programme is concerned *there is now nothing left on the agenda sheet of world history before the return of Christ*. Jesus has overcome death and ascended to his Father. He has given his Spirit to every one of his

[1] I John 2: 18.

followers. The next item on the agenda will be his return! Thus we are in the "last hour", and as such are to be found faithfully living for Christ in daily work and employment, and extending his kingdom in the lives of others.

Meanwhile the battle rages. Let no prospective follower of Christ be under any illusions. It *is* battle, even if our weapons are the invisible weapons of prayer and of the Spirit, and even if the conquest is an invisible invasion of love accomplished in lives and personalities. In some parts of the world there are tremendous – some would even say unprecedented – spiritual advances being made. Elsewhere we may be faced with a holding operation; with the day of small things, where the tide of evil is in and where Christians are called to be "Canutes" – faithful in teaching the ones and twos, secure in the timeless assurance that comes reverberating to them across the centuries, that "The gates of hell shall not prevail against my Church".[1]

I used to imagine that this promise of Jesus implied a picture of the Church under attack from the forces of darkness, desperately surviving against bitter odds, miraculously staving off defeat, limping from crisis to crisis. I now think differently. Crises there may be, but the biblical picture is that of *hell itself under storm from a militant, invading Church* – armed with the Word of God and motivated by the love of Christ. And in the forefront, a Figure on a white horse. We do not need to inquire as to his identity. We know him by a single glance at his hands and feet. We know him by the difference his very presence makes to everything. The

[1] Matthew 16: 18.

inscription upon his Person removes any remaining vestige of uncertainty. It reads, "King of Kings, and Lord of Lords." That tells me all. The past is atoned for. The advantage in the immediate present is weighted in our favour. And tomorrow belongs to us!